Eleanor Bird has been involved in children's work leadership since she was twelve and in full-time ministry since the age of 21. She has led children's venues for New Wine and run workshops and seminars for leaders across the UK. Previously the Children's Pastor at King's Church Amersham, Eleanor moved to Greater Manchester in 2012 to join the leadership team at St Chad's Romiley. As their Head of Children and Youth Ministry, she now oversees all ministries with two- to 19-year-olds, and is tasked with cultivating a vision and culture that releases and equips God's people to be who he created them to be.

Together with her husband Paul, Eleanor has a passion to see all of God's children (whatever their age) step into the calling God has put on their lives, through encountering his Holy Spirit and cultivating lives that are centred on pursuing him. Eleanor's heart has been captured by God's church, and her dream is to see churches function as united families that include everyone in the journey of life-transforming faith.

Text copyright © Eleanor Bird 2015
The author asserts the moral right to be identified as the author of this work

Published by
The Bible Reading Fellowship
15 The Chambers, Vineyard
Abingdon, OX14 3FE
United Kingdom
Tel: +44 (0)1865 319700
Email: enquiries@brf.org.uk
Website: www.brf.org.uk
BRF is a Registered Charity

ISBN 978 0 85746 112 4
First published 2015
10 9 8 7 6 5 4 3 2 1 0
All rights reserved

Acknowledgements
Scripture taken from *The Message*. Copyright © 1993, 1994, 1995, 1996, 2000,
2001, 2002. Used by permission of NavPress Publishing Group.

Scripture quotations taken from the Holy Bible, New Living Translation, copyright
© 1996, 2004, 2007, 2013. Used by permission of Tyndale House Publishers, Inc.,
Carol Stream, Illinois 60188. All rights reserved.

Scripture quotations marked NCV are taken from the New Century Version®,
copyright © 2005 by Thomas Nelson, Inc. Used by permission. All rights reserved.

Scripture quotations taken from The Holy Bible, New International Version
(Anglicised edition) copyright © 1973, 1978, 1984, 2011 by Biblica (formerly
International Bible Society). Used by permission of Hodder & Stoughton
Publishers, an Hachette UK company. All rights reserved. 'NIV' is a registered
trade mark of Biblica (formerly International Bible Society). UK trademark
number 1448790.

Every effort has been made to trace and contact copyright owners for material
used in this resource. We apologise for any inadvertent omissions or errors, and
would ask those concerned to contact us so that full acknowledgement can be
made in the future.

A catalogue record for this book is available from the British Library

Printed and bound by CPI Group (UK) Ltd, Croydon CR0 4YY

BLENDED
A CALL TO REIMAGINE OUR CHURCH FAMILY

Rethinking how we can
be church together

ELEANOR BIRD

Acknowledgements

To God: This is all for you, Dad! You put this book in my heart and I will be forever humbled and honoured that you chose to give these words to me first. Thank you for including me in your plans, for adopting me as your child, for choosing me to be your friend and equipping me for the calling you have given me. Without you I'm nothing, and with you I am more than I could ever have imagined. I praise you, Dad, for I was fearfully and wonderfully made.

To Paul: You constantly hold me to higher standards and see in me the potential for greatness. Thank you, my love. Thank you for putting up with the stress, tension and confusion that life sometimes causes in me, and for continually reminding me of my purpose and calling. You don't just help to keep me on track; you hold my head up when I can't, and cheer me on to run the race.

To my parents, sister and family: You brought me up to believe that I could change the world and taught me the true meaning of family. Thank you. Thank you for the love, support and encouragement you have surrounded me with all my life. Through your love of God and excitement to see me fly, I have learnt to soar on eagle's wings. Together we make a very special family, and I love you.

To Rachel: Thank you for your patience, time, support and poking! Without you, this project wouldn't have been possible. Your unwavering friendship and the passionate way you walk beside me have fundamentally changed my heart and for that, I thank God for you.

To Olivia and all the BRF team: Thank you for giving me this opportunity, and for sharing your expertise and time with me. Your ability to see in me the possibility of a book has truly blessed my heart and given me a voice I didn't know I had.

And finally I want to say thank you to my crowd of witnesses: Elaine, Kathleen, Jenny, Pauline, Julian, Ant, Sarah, Jill, Katie and all the friends who have been cheering me on. To my church families and their leaders (David and St Andrew's, Paul and King's Church, Richard and St Chad's), who have given me freedom and time to experiment and invest in what God was saying to me, thank you! You have kept me believing in myself and trusting that I do have something to say. Your listening ears, prayer, and support have kept me going. I wouldn't have wanted to do this without you.

This book is dedicated to two incredible leaders. Through their friendship and ministry I saw God truly become the author and perfector of my faith. Valerie and Kent, you opened up your home to me, shared your ideas and life with me, and above all gave me the opportunities I needed to discover the leader God made me to be. Thank you!

Contents

The call

Appendices

[A love letter]

Dear Church

You are amazing. There is something about you that means you are so much more than the sum of the human parts that make you. There is this heavenly invasion into the very fabric of who you are that makes you completely attractive to me. I can't get enough! I can't stop dreaming about all that you are and all that you can become.

You have so much more to give.

So many people spend their energy organising you, timetabling you, and getting you to fit with their plans, when, at your best, you are a living, breathing mechanism from God that brings out the best in his children.

You amaze me! You point me to the greatness of God and enable me to discover the greatness of me (the greatness God put in me). The more I work with you, Church, the more I get to know you, the more I want to understand what makes you so like God. You're creative, powerful and strong. You're misunderstood, misrepresented and misused. So many people throughout history have used you to bring control; they have used you to gain power for themselves, not release power from heaven. How can that be? How can humanity's free will change such a beautiful gift from their loving father?!

I love you, Church, and I want to be with you. I want to use you to your full potential, as a tool not only for change but also for freedom. I want to experience you in all of God's glory—

9

seeing you so expansive with energy that all people are released into their full potential too.

If you reach your full potential, Church, then I think God's people will too. And that's worth aiming for. Isn't it?

Love
Eleanor xx

This is the rock on which I will put together my church, a church so expansive with energy that not even the gates of hell will be able to keep it out.

MATTHEW 16:18, *The Message*

The heart

Blended Church is about investigating a new way of being God's family. It's about us, as church leaders and as ministry leaders: letting God challenge us, opening up our processes and programmes again to him, and dreaming afresh about the future. For all of that, we need to align our heart with our Father, making sure his love is entwined with ours.

Chapter 1

Loving church

The first thing we are called to do is love. God loved and that meant we lived. Jesus continued that message on the day

> We love each other because he loved us first.
> 1 JOHN 4:19, NLT

he rose to heaven. He gave us one job to do before he left to be at his father's side: love people enough to share his good news with them.

As church leaders and ministry leaders, our role to love God's people has to start with loving his whole church. This book is intended to be the beginning of a new journey for us. It's the journey of asking the questions that God has for us today and following where those answers lead. God wants to lead us to love his whole church, as much as his individual children. He wants his body of Christ to be an accurate reflection of his son Jesus. He wants to empower us as his leaders, to be agents of change, and open to him as he expands the capacity of our hearts and our ministries to fit the fullness of his love inside them.

We can do that in many different ways. We're all designed differently, called to different things, purposed for different parts of God's glory, but we

> Guard your heart above all else, for it determines the course of your life.
> PROVERBS 4:23, NLT

all have something in common—the way our humanity works. We are heart people. Jesus told us that words from our heart can get us into trouble; that's why we're told to guard them. When we set out on the journey to build God's church, we need to make sure our heart is lined up with his. That way, our actions will be an accurate reflection of our Father, and in line with his life-giving love. If the words we speak from our heart define us and set the course of our life, then the church we build, powered by our heart for God's people, will do the same.

Loving church

Church is alive and well, living and breathing, and it's here to stay, in all its multi-ethnic, multifaceted, multiformatted glory. Over the span of my life I have fallen in love with church. When I was little, I was taught the classic Sunday school phrase: 'Church isn't the building; it's the people,' and of course that is true, but, like each one of us, there is always more to uncover and more God-given potential than we first see. Falling in love with church has been an intriguing process—first, working out exactly what it is that has captured my heart and second, discovering why God designed my heart to be right for this process in the first place.

I grew up in a mixed faith family. What I mean is that when I was young, my mum was a Christian and my dad wasn't, and the tension between those two camps has shaped my entire life. My mum made sure that God, church and faith were natural to me; God's presence was understood and invited into our home and therefore my life. My dad taught me something very different. He taught me that a relationship with God isn't something you inherit or 'fall into'; he taught me that if I wanted what my mum had, I'd need to choose it for myself.

By the time I was six I had worked out that I had

a choice: go to church with mum, or stay at home with dad. Church meant friends and fun, and I chose it a lot of the time, but home with dad meant having his attention 100 per cent, no getting dressed, films and chocolate, and sometimes I would choose that instead.

It was actually my dad who made the change. He didn't want me to choose home over church, to choose him over God, I guess, and so he decided to go with my mum and my sister and me to church.

By the time I was ten I had decided for myself that Jesus' being my mum's best friend wasn't good enough for me, so I chose him for myself, and accepted all he had to offer. Our free will and choice is often edited out of the way we communicate the gospel to each other, especially for those of us brought up with the reality of God's existence in their day-to-day lives from an early age. Without a deep-rooted and empowered understanding of the choice we have in the matter of our salvation, we are missing out on the security and certainty that deciding to follow Jesus gives us. Without knowing I had to choose Jesus for myself, and continually choose him, I wouldn't have developed a faith of my own.

I wouldn't have been able to watch as God dug my own foundations and I wouldn't have learnt to let God alone define who I was. My story became whole when I mixed for myself choice and God's existence as my daily reality.

> If anyone belongs to Christ, there is a new creation. The old things have gone; everything is made new!
> 2 CORINTHIANS 5:17, NCV

When the reality of God's existence inspired in me the transformational choice of choosing him, I became a new creation, in my own right.

What we discover as we unpack the knowledge of our choice in the matter of our salvation is God's choice too. He chose us, he sent his son to choose us, and he chooses to empower us to be the fullness of his design for us, as we walk out in faith, with him.

Long before we first heard of Christ and got our hopes up, he had his eye on us, had designs on us for glorious living, part of the overall purpose he is working out in everything and everyone.
EPHESIANS 1:11–12,
The Message

I now choose daily to be my mix of God as reality and choice, and one of the many things God has blessed my eyes with seeing is my dad making the same choice as I did a year later. He is now, in his own unique way, whole in that world-changing mix of God and choice.

What we're building

There is the same choice for the church. In its mix of God as a daily reality and humanity's own individual and corporate choices, it is pursuing and discovering its full potential. The church I want to be a part of is one that doesn't just live in the reality of God, but with every breath and moment chooses him and his ways. God says, in his word, 'Love me, and walk in my ways.' When we, as individuals or as the

I command you today: Love God, your God. Walk in his ways. Keep his command-ments, regulations, and rules so that you will live, really live, live exuberantly, blessed by God, your God, in the land you are about to enter and possess.
DEUTERONOMY 30:16,
The Message

church, have those two things on our 'to do list', then we are on our journey into the fullness and glory of our godly potential. If that's not our aim, if we are serving other goals, then are we really sure the direction we're headed in is the right one? God makes it really simple. Do things his way and the life we'll get in return won't just bless us, but the land, the people and locations he's calling us to as well.

How often do we substitute individual and corporate

choice for format and formula? How often do we, as leaders, feel the pressure of bringing in new and funky ways of doing things, just because they're different? Format and formula burnout is real! And it's not just for the leaders—all of our church family members suffer from it too.

Getting your 'own ministry' is a landmark many of us are aiming for. For me this was my first full-time children's ministry position. When I got there, I arrived with so many ideas and expectations that I confused myself. Before I'd even started I was lost, especially as I found that my new leaders, children, congregation and bosses had ideas and expectations too. Discovering, with God, his way for me to run, create and develop ministry has been my key to avoiding format burnout. All the good ideas in the world are worth nothing if we don't get them from God. All the changes in the world won't impact on people if they are not instigated by him. Paul tells us that we are the body of Christ. Over time the importance of the body of Christ hasn't changed—scholars don't tell us that we should aim to be the slingshot of David or the staff of Moses. We are still called to be the body of Christ along with the rest of God's people. What does change is what the body, or parts of the body, are directed to do.

My body and my DNA will never fundamentally change; I will, however, do many different things throughout my life. In the same way, my ministry, the church I am a part of building (whether for one age bracket or all of them) should never fundamentally change. It should, however, be intrinsically linked to the brain (God)

I want you to think about how all this makes you more significant, not less. A body isn't just a single part blown up into something huge. It's all the similar parts arranged and functioning together... As it is we see that God has carefully placed each part of the body right where he wanted it.
1 CORINTHAINS 12:18–20, *THE MESSAGE*

and move forward as he directs. We are all called into the building industry by our Father; we are all called to be active members of his body—building his church, for his people and constructed together with his people.

What we're all called to

Several years ago I was at a Christian conference. It was the beginning of another week in a tent, with mud and no proper showers. I was prepared for a week of getting closer to God and getting closer to nature. It was the first night, so I was all excited about what God would do with the week I'd set aside, and I was expecting some big changes. For me, this type of conference hasn't always been a 'mountain top' experience but has always been a time where I have experienced change and refining. So, I was standing near the front on the end of a row (my seat of choice at events like this), quickly getting lost in the atmosphere, the worship and God. All of a sudden someone came up to me and said, 'God says, "You are called to something beautiful." I don't know what that means but I hope you do.' Stunned, I only nodded as she ran off but in that minute or so of exchange God tugged at my heartstrings and puzzled my brain. I had no idea what she meant, or more importantly, what God meant. There was only one thing certain in my mind—he definitely wasn't referring to what I'd look like after a week of camping!

It was a month before the full revelation of those six words hit my heart. God's church is designed to be *beautiful* and, as a lover of it and a member of it, my calling is to be part of the process of making it, keeping it, and encouraging it to be *beautiful*. For me the definition of that is simple—when God's people gather together, understanding who he is, and are committed to doing what he wants in his power, then they, his church, are truly beautiful in heaven's eyes. Or, as Ephesians 2:10 says, 'For we are God's handiwork, created in Christ Jesus to do good works, which God prepared for us in advance' (NIV).

> For God saved us and called us to live a holy life. He did this, not because we deserved it, but because that was his plan from before the beginning of time—to show us his grace through Christ Jesus.
> 2 TIMOTHY 1:9, NLT

I guess the reason I am writing this all down is simply because I want to share the blessings I have received and say to you: 'You are called to something beautiful too.'

This book is about exploring how we do that together, how we build our church as a beautiful family. There may not be all the answers you're looking for in this book, but God first wants us to align our hearts and minds, our thought processes and the perspectives that lead us to make decisions, before getting down to the specific details of what his church, in our individual lives and contexts, looks like.

A prayer

Dad, you are the best planner I know. You set every star in the sky, manage every change of season and orchestrate every beat of every heart you placed so gently in your children's bodies. You blow my mind with how complex your creation is, and yet you comfort my heart with how simply you explain things to me.

We love your church. We are so grateful for the people you have surrounded us with and places you have asked us to live. We want to be a part of your plans for our church family. We want to follow your lead and bring beauty to every aspect of your creation.

As we set aside this time and turn our thoughts to you, would you grow in us the capacity to do your work in your strength, to lead in your ways and follow in your Son's journey. Would you empower us to love your church to the point where each one of its members actively loves and follows you. Amen

The
vision

Blended Church is church in a new way, with a
new set of values and ideas. This section is designed
to share the vision of what these values and ideas are,
and how we, as leaders, can adopt them, grow and
develop our churches through our own unique way of
pursuing God's vision for his people.

Chapter 2

A Blended Church

As you now know, choice was a massive part of my childhood. God used it to shape me and my faith, and, through those experiences, he taught me the reality and joy of choice and free will. Through his grace, he has given me the passion to share with others the knowledge that they too have choices. Not all children will have the joy of seeing their dad choosing God, but if they are equipped with this knowledge they can see the transformation in the many other people around them.

The second defining gift God gave me as I grew up was a large family. I had four generations of my family around for much of my early life and, from the time I was ten years old, we have been meeting once a year for the mother of all picnics. I have continuously witnessed the joy and tension of family dynamics through mini golf, sharing food, playing boules, cricket and conversation. In my home church I saw many of the same values established and never really realised how precious they were until I encountered churches that didn't feel the same.

Through the ministries God has called me to and the places he has taken me, I have visited and been a part of several different churches and noticed that many fit into one of two camps.

'Camp one': The church that sees being all together as a sacrifice, one they are sometimes not willing to make. They have all-age activities as little as possible because they want their adult time with God when he can really move, their youth time with God when he is more relevant and their kid time with God when he can make most sense.

'Camp two': The church that doesn't mind not meeting with God as much if it means being all together, that loves the opportunity to do activities at a different level or pitch, if it means everyone is included and doesn't expect God to move in power or be transformational in that setting.

For a while I was left with one question. Why do our expectations of church, and of our time corporately with God, have to change because other people are in the room? For example, why is a family service ever seen as a sacrifice, even if we are happy and willing to make that sacrifice?

My family, especially the men, take boules very seriously at our family picnics. When my soon-to-be-husband came on the scene at the family picnic there was definitely a moment of thinking, 'Hey, newcomer, do you understand the gravity of joining us?' (and by that they meant the game, not the family). The irony was that, however seriously my family took the game, everyone was allowed to play. There was no training round, no standard to achieve, no age you had to be before you could join in the 'proper event'. The youngest cousins played, the talented members and the not so talented. There was a genuine fight to win but a joy in playing too. Just because smaller children were playing didn't mean the adults didn't try their best. Just because there was a newcomer didn't mean they stopped using our own unique brand of family banter. They simply included each new person and explained the jokes as they went along.

Why can't church be like that? Why can't we expect to have the best morning of our life, achieve the deepest depths of revelation and understanding, while including newcomers and all ages? Jesus didn't give the Sermon on the Mount one day and the newcomers' version the next morning, followed by a kids' tea and talk in the afternoon. He spoke to everyone together and that didn't mean that everyone got it straight away. It meant everyone shared in the experience of receiving, investigating and living out his revelation as they lived alongside each other. Jesus operated out of the distinct conviction that it is entirely possible to have a deep encounter with God with all ages in the room, in the congregation, or in this case on the mountain side. So, if Jesus operated out of that belief, why shouldn't his body? Why shouldn't our church family?

The Greek word for 'church' means 'called-out ones'. Matthew shows us there are four clear characteristics to Jesus' priorities, for us as his body, to be God's called-out people.

> The Greek word *ekklesia* is translated in most places as 'church'. The word *ekklesia* is found 115 times in the New Testament. In Greek the word *ekklesia* originally meant 'a called-out assembly of citizens summoned by the crier'.
>
> Strong's Exhaustive Concordance & Dictionary, number: G1577, www.blueletterbible.org

- Direct revelation from God of who he is ('Bless you, you didn't get the answer out of books')
- Openness to accept who God says we are ('I'm going to tell you who you are')
- A commitment to following his Father's plan ('I will put together my church, a church so expansive with energy that not even the gates of hell will stand')

- An acceptance of the gifts of his kingdom that he offers to equip us ('You will have complete and free access to all of God's kingdom').

Jesus came back, 'God bless you, Simon, son of Jonah! You didn't get that answer out of books or from teachers. My Father in heaven, God himself, let you in on this secret of who I really am. And now I'm going to tell you who you are, really are. You are Peter, a rock. This is the rock on which I will put together my church, a church so expansive with energy that not even the gates of hell will be able to keep it out. And that's not all. You will have complete and free access to God's kingdom, keys to open any and every door: no more barriers between heaven and earth, earth and heaven.'
MATTHEW 16:17–19,
The Message

We are a family and, for me, part of the journey we are on is learning how to be a Blended one. All four of these priorities can be achieved in our separate age groups, and should be in many different situations, but we should also expect to achieve them together. As God's chosen people, we need to choose not only him but each other too. Blended Church is about being a church that functions as a family first, that chooses to be the whole body before a specific mission arm or age group.

For years, many of us have been stuck in the expectation of adding 'all age' to the existing framework of our churches. It's a frustrating and often thankless task that can regularly result in people being either unhappy about what currently exists, or dissatisfied because of what doesn't. Having church groups that are segregated by age has been a choice many churches have made in order to speed up the process of discipleship. The hope was that if the adults did 'their thing' in isolation they would see more fruit much more quickly, and the same went for meeting as kids' groups and youth groups. Splitting up held the promise of 'getting where we're going' faster. These choices have meant we have stopped aiming to function as a family above all else, and instead have prioritised specific or segregated ministries, or, even worse, the 'results' of our ministries. The problem is that in trying to get 'there' faster, we've forgotten that the point was to get there together.

We need to shift the dynamics and change our perspective on being a church. Instead of occasionally investing in the together part of our journey, we need to start from the perspective of being a family, blended into one team, before starting off on the journey together; and for that, we need to leave segregation behind.

The following looks at being Jesus' body in two different ways: a beautiful family, and a prism.

A beautiful family: being God's church is aiming to be a beautiful family in three different directions

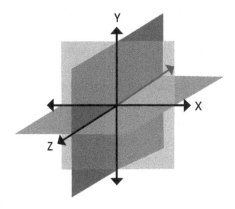

- Direction one (side-to-side—think timeline): including all ages, loving being together and loving being apart too.

The point is that we want to love people at the age they are now, not what they will be in future.

- Direction two (front to back, running from the outside to the inside of our churches): never feeling in or out, but being together on the journey of getting closer to Jesus. Putting a value on being on the journey, not on how far along each person is.

- Direction three (vertical, heaven to earth and back again): actively blending heaven and earth. Expecting God to move, expecting to see the effects of his power on earth, and expecting that we have a part to play in his plans for the world and our community.

When you take a step back and put all the three directions together, the lines our beautiful family draws create something earth-shattering. You see that from every angle our 'blended lines' mark out the cross, the ultimate sign of Jesus, and now the ultimate sign of our family. Let's face it, looking like Jesus from every angle has to be the most beautiful thing there is.

I explained this to my church using ribbons. As people held out the two horizontal lines and a helium balloon carried the third one up to the roof of our church there was a tangible joy as we saw for ourselves how many different angles you can see the cross from. That's what church should be to our communities—a source of joy as they see the many different angles of Jesus' cross.

A prism: being God's church is letting God release his full spectrum of colour in our family

ONE GOD
shining
his light

To create
ALL THE
COLOURS
of his
children

Through his
ONE SON

Before a guy called Isaac Newton was around, everyone thought light was colourless. He thought differently and, with perseverance and science, he managed to prove it. He found that when white light passes through a prism, it is refracted into its component colours—all the colours of the rainbow. God's design for us is to be his body (and by that I mean his hands and feet, eyes and ears, on earth) and this is like the process of refracting light. The way I see it is: our ONE GOD shines his light (his power, anointing, love, plans) through his ONE SON, which produces ALL THE COLOURS of his children. We've spent too long seeing church as one colour, when really we were a rainbow all along.

In our aim to be that one colour, we split up so that we don't contaminate each other, but actually our beauty is in being different together. In us, God creates distinctive people, different and unique but from the same place, his heart. As God's family, our job is to be as much like

Jesus as we can be, together and separately. Loving all the differences we exhibit, not minding how close people are to Jesus and deliberately looking for heaven on earth.

A new word for a new hope

I prayed for over three years for what to call the family services at the church where I worked first. 'Family service' had a bad reputation all over our area, 'all age' seemed dull, and every acronym I came up with seemed weird and forgettable. 'Am I meant to claim an old misused title or start something new?' was the question I circled around for years. That's when God gave me 'Blended'.

It wasn't a word that was commonly used or associated with church, and the secular, social-work world was starting to use it for the new 'format' of family that society was creating. No more was a nuclear family the standard; we were moving to a new 'norm' of family and that was being described as 'blended'. What a great meaning to claim for God! And so Blended was born, at least in my own heart— and from there I have been developing the thinking, vision and language that goes with it, and the programme, format and ideas that are informed by it.

The blender effect

Dear friends, since God loved us that much, we surely ought to love each other… God is love, and all who live in love live in God, and God lives in them… Such love has no fear, because perfect love expels all fear.

1 JOHN 4:11, 16, 18, NLT

Before we get on to what being Blended looks like and the building it takes, it's worth quickly acknowledging the fear that many face when Blended comes on the horizon. It's called the 'blender effect'! Most of us have lots of different

30

favourite foods. I myself love roast dinners, ice cream and red wine but if I put all of them in a blender, I wouldn't be multiplying the joy; I'd be destroying it. When we talk about blending our family together, often people are scared that the joy will be destroyed in that too. Sure, we're all God's favourite, but if we all mix together, won't we all be lost?

This anxiety can be in individuals as well as in congregations. We may be concerned because we come to church to meet with God without distraction and have him deal with issues in us, or because the service is the way we like church services to be. It highlights the difference between being a consumer of church and a contributor to church. The blender effect is about having a fear in us that sees being Blended as not giving us the opportunities we need or want. The result is that often people end up wanting a segregated church. Church becomes more about what I can get and therefore how I get it, rather than who we are and how we can grow together.

The skill of a chef is in their ability to make many different flavours sing, all at once; the skill of an artist is to use many colours to make one beautiful thing. God is more skilled than these and though our fear of being Blended is real and important to voice, it's founded on the lie that God would let us get lost in his crowd; that he meets our needs on our terms, individually and corporately; that church is about what we can get from it, not give to it; that God would let our joy in him be taken by another. Spoken out like that, our fear of the blender effect starts to look a lot less important than before.

The way to conquer this fear is simple. Confess it to God every time it rises up in you, in your family, or your church, and let God's strength enable you to press on into him regardless—trusting that being a Blended body is what you are called to be, and is better than a separate, segregated one.

How to start building in the beauty

It's all very well believing in this stuff, agreeing with the idea of one Blended family, one church, but it's natural to feel that we need to know what this vision might taste like before going and changing the recipe for how we fundamentally function. Before going further and looking at several of the big areas of being Blended, we first need to understand that our thinking needs to shift. There are four key values to Blended Church that challenge most of us and examine the current ways we think about church. Before moving forward, we need to accept and have come to our own conclusions on these four values.

Stop calling it work: We readily speak of children's work and children's workers. Yet if we started calling our morning service, or our small/mid-week/cluster/cell groups the 'adult work' in the church, then I'm guessing the adults would start to be offended. If, instead of pastors and vicars, we called our church leaders 'adult workers', I think the tone would change in the adults around us. Language is incredibly important, and although none of us wants to put labels on people, our words do end up labelling them. So we need to think through what we say, how we say it, and to ensure that it is equal on all counts and intentionally part of the overall design for our family.

We need to shift the culture of our churches to see that everything we do is connected and is ministry. After my first two years as a kids' worker I got my title changed to children's pastor. This was simply because I believed the children deserved a pastor. In that church all 'adult workers' were pastors and so it fitted with our church family's language, and accurately expressed my role and the value it had in the overall community. If we are going to blend together, we need to start by sharing the same language. We need to understand that language is one of the biggest pillars we have for upholding and communicating value. We need to root out the things that show evidence of where larger value has been placed on one demographic of our family over another. Of course, it is not just the language we need to change but the opinions or beliefs that created the inequality of value in the first place. However, language is a good place to start, and changing it in our churches will often stimulate the conversations we need to have with its people.

Another example of this is in the language we use to describe our activities. On a Sunday morning the usual title for what the adults are doing is church, but we can call what the children and youth are doing anything from an abstract word or acronym, for which potentially no one can remember the reason, to things like 'club' or 'group'. That difference in language points to an inequality in how each programme is viewed. We don't call our adult church service a club, because it's not one. We use the word church because it communicates more fully the opportunity for discipleship, encounter with God and worship. All of God's children deserve opportunities for that and so along with changing my job title, I changed our Sunday morning kids' groups to tots' church, mini church and kids' church (in my current job I also changed the youth name to youth church). It best illustrated that on a Sunday morning each age group was seeking the same God, the same experiences and focusing on the same vision. It gave language to the fact that on our mornings when we all met separately, we were in fact a church of churches; a church family, expressed over several programmes, and it brought a linguistic equality to the Sunday morning structure that would develop into an equality in the vision and value of each group, age range and programme.

Cohesion is vital to blending. We have one God and his three expressions (Father, Son and Holy Spirit) work seamlessly, both together and apart. They blend because they are from the same source, and the language we use to explain and surround them is equal. People are not work. The ways in which we reach out to them, disciple them and love them should not be communicated in such a way that it sounds task-driven and effortful. Ministry is more than a job, and for many it's outside of their work-life anyway. It's the lifestyle that God has called us to. Let's communicate that instead, and let's show our equal value of people in the way we communicate the ministries, programmes and leaders they have.

Welcome influence: As leaders, it's a painful thing to admit, but we need to surrender our kingdoms and share them with others. Blended Church means giving others a voice in your land. Those of us who have clear boundaries (like 'children', 'youth', 'students', 'adults', 'families') need to be actively seeking and accepting the influence of other ways of doing things that represent our family as a whole. We need to be giving others a voice in our groups and 'kingdoms' because they are part of our family, not because they attend most regularly or shout the loudest.

I know being a family and being a church is more than this, but for a minute let's separate out the way we spend our Sunday mornings from the rest. If we want to have the option of meaningful, spirit-filled Sunday mornings together, we need to find ways of merging, and the way to do this is to share. The ways that help our adults engage with God should be seen and used in the children's programme—partly because they'll be adults soon, but mainly because it means they'll understand better the adult service when they find themselves in it. It also starts to create the ground for respect and shows how we can empower our children to uphold the adults in their church family. The music the youth love should be used by the adults; the teaching programme the children are following should be covered by the teenagers and adults too, and vice versa. The adult sermon series should be taught in the youth discipleship programme and kids' church. Cross-pollination, rooted in sharing the journey, is vital; it builds a common language, a shared joy and a basis for deep-rooted respect.

Why? Because being together on the journey is more important than how fast we get to the finish line. Using a previously labelled 'adult' song with children takes longer because we have to spend time learning it first, but the joy of singing one song across all the ages is worth it. Jesus told us adults to become like small children, and that can include learning alongside them. Not all adults in our churches have been coming along since they were children. Sharing

> For an answer Jesus called over a child, whom he stood in the middle of the room, and said, 'I'm telling you, once and for all, that unless you return to square one and start over like children, you're not even going to get a look at the kingdom, let alone get in. Whoever becomes simple and elemental again, like this child, will rank high in God's kingdom. What's more, when you receive the childlike on my account, it's the same as receiving me.'
>
> MATTHEW 18:3, *The Message*

the simple truths, going through the stories 'the adults will already know' might just bring joy, truth and understanding in ways we had forgotten adults can access. Who better to teach us how to be like children than children?

We need to dig out the competitive spirit from between our different generations and start them working together, and apart, for the same goals.

When we're apart: Train for when we're together—not necessarily overtly, but in the culture of your groups, the way the leaders interact and the way people are listened to and guided. We need to be training all our people in how to seek God together.

We need to change our perspective on what we feel when we split into our different (age, preference, timetabled) groups. Right now, often we are relieved to be doing things in our group, loving the opportunity to do things 'our way' and not having to compromise; we may be thinking of these times as bliss, easy and achievable. I heard a children's leader once say: 'Give me your children from 0 to 11 and I'll get them to be where they [spiritually] need to be.' Haven't we all felt like that at times?

I'm not saying that feeling like that is bad. It's understandable, but if we live for the times when we're apart how will we ever be happy together? Instead, we need to see our times apart as joyful, wonderful experiences and expressions of part of our family and use them to work together to be one cohesive and loving Blended team.

As an example, in worship we need to train each other how to worship for different lengths of time so that adults don't feel they've missed out if there are only a couple of songs when they are used to many songs normally, and we need to ensure the children don't get bored in extended times, and equip them with strategies to help themselves in these times too. We need to train each other to worship to songs we don't like, when words we don't understand are being used or when the music isn't our 'style'. Why? So that when we're all together, our worship is still authentic and pleasing to God!

This understanding needs to start with the mindset of the leaders, and not of the congregation. If we lead with this heart and develop our individual groups and ministries from this perspective, then the format will follow and ultimately be blendable.

When we're together: We need to experiment and create signposts that include everyone. We're going to look at worship, teaching and ministry in more detail later, which will explain this idea more practically, but we need to find ways of explaining what we're doing as we go along that includes all.

On any given morning with our church family, it's not just the children who don't know 'everything' (if knowing it all is ever actually possible); there will be plenty of adults, visitors and others who don't know the jargon and what's next on the running order, and that can be alienating. Explaining what we're doing, why we're doing it, and how God fits into it as we go along, through simple verbal, visual and kinaesthetic signposts helps everyone, even the most initiated of our family members.

Signposting is taking everything you have considered, all the little decisions you made, and the questions you pondered beforehand, and making them public for all to see and understand. When it comes to the different elements of your programme, displaying an image that is recognisable, a Bible verse or definition that gives a bit of insight while you chat through the session and the sections helps everyone. For adults and those whose minds might wander from the audio explanation, there is something to read, something that gets their mind working. For those who prefer the visual or can't yet read, the picture is something they'll learn to associate with what is going on— even just the colour can become your signpost. By being consistent with these signposts, you can build up a visual, audio and literary language that doesn't just keep everyone on track, but enables them to join in more fully with their family around them.

It costs us nothing to change our language from jargon to signposts. It takes thinking through and planning, but what we lose in extra preparation time we gain in family time. Instead of 'The reading is taken from Ephesians 6', why can't we say: 'There was this guy called Paul and he wrote letters to churches all over the place. One letter was to Ephesus and in it he wanted to share with them how God can protect us. This is what he wrote...'? That would take only 15 seconds more and communicate to everyone in a way that didn't baby them or insult them but, instead, grouped them together through understanding and knowledge.

The risk is that we can end up creating a whole new jargon for our family, which is why all we do needs to be informed and rooted in our Blended heart and vision. When consistently done, signposting takes our way of normally doing things and makes it inclusive and missional. It means no one is left behind, and everyone can keep up. It doesn't add hours on to a programme or cause us more work; it simply utilises what we already know as leaders and equips our family with truth and understanding. Being together isn't about making wise compromises; it's about cultivating good communication.

The purpose of church

Throughout the next five chapters of this book we are going to look at the purpose and values of being God's called-out people: why he chose to design us to be in relationship with him and with each other, and how we can build and grow our church families in response to that. The original title for this book was 'The Building Blocks of Church' and, although this title doesn't really fit anymore, there is still part of this idea in play.

It's in Christ that we find out who we are and what we are living for. Long before we first heard of Christ and got our hopes up, he had his eye on us, had designs on us for glorious living, part of the overall purpose he is working out in everything and everyone.
EPHESIANS 1:11, *The Message*

What is key, however, is not that we seek to find the format that works best, or the material we can quickly adapt, but that we all take the time to let God shape our questions and our dreams, and ultimately our entire way of thinking. As we hear about the different areas, ideas and aspects of church in its widest context, we need to keep our own context in mind: the people we are called to and the locations we have been placed in.

Our purpose comes from whose body we are. We can share our ideas, stories and dreams as much as we like but if we don't allow Jesus to determine who we are individually and corporately, then we've missed the point. This book was originally going to be about a practical equipping, but God changed that and reminded me that we are to do things his way from a place of seeking him and relying on our daily bread. It will look a lot like doing things 'our way', as long as we do them with him.

Let's remember our four key values as we move from this place to consider again all the 'blocks' God is giving us to build with, as we set out to discover his design for us.

1. Church isn't work, so don't call it that.
2. Let's give everyone an equal influence over how things fit in our family because we really do value each of our members.
3. When we're apart, we can be training for when we're together.
4. When we're together, we can make the most of the opportunity to keep experimenting and explaining.

Chapter 3

The opportunities in a Blended Church

As God's Blended Church we need to engage with the different ways we can think about church, using our understanding of why God made us to be in families. We are God's beautiful and Blended family, with the purpose and dream to be the active and God-connected body of Christ on earth. If we can understand what church is and how God designed it to function, then we are better placed to know how to go about building the Blended Church we are called to be. So, let's first look deeper into the 'what' of church, before moving on to the 'how'.

Church is a God-given ministry of opportunities, and being a Blended Church is about growing together and

> Therefore go and make disciples of all nations.
> MATTHEW 28:19, NIV

gathering others. I heard the great commission retranslated from 'Go and make disciples,' to 'While you're going, bring others along for the ride,' and the change in phrasing really struck me. This change in expression is helpful for us as we look at the purpose of ministry inside and outside of the church and exactly what we, as church families, should be focusing on.

As God's children, we are people on a journey, walking towards God, into deeper discipleship and maturity, and, as Blended Churches, we need to invest in that journey. We also need to be bringing others along with us, investing in them, including them on our journey and, ideally, helping them excel as we all travel together 'to the ends of the earth' (Acts 1:8). Instead of our ministries being about events and groups, they should be about building a set of opportunities, aimed at the people we feel called to be reaching, as well as those who are already in our church families.

When I was little, I was taught that every Christian had to care about all of the ministries of God; that there were whole lists of roles, jobs and missions in the Bible that God would give me. As I grew up, somewhere in my learning I confused being passionate about the whole of God's church and being called to the whole of God's church. That confusion led me to having a secret I felt really guilty about: I had no interest in mission! It's not that I didn't want it to happen or for other people to invest in it—I just really didn't want it to be me. Sure, I wanted to see the world and go to Africa, but it wasn't for the 'right reasons'; I just wanted to see more of what God had made. I greatly valued finding God's lost sheep; I just didn't want to be on the search team.

Just after I got married, a friend was asking me about what kind of a team my husband, Paul, and I were going to make. It was in this conversation God corrected a few of my childhood misunderstandings; he's good like that. I told my friend what Paul was passionate about; how discovering God as an adult had made him want to work with teenagers so they didn't have to face those years without God. I was explaining that his testimony of finding God when life was going really well (he'd just met me, so why wouldn't it?) had led him to question 'How do we, as a church, do that?' Introducing people to God when they are in a time of crisis was one thing, but what about all those who were happy, who, in their understanding of life wanted for nothing? How do we explain to them that they might just need Jesus? I then went on to talk about me, my passion for Christians, for growing leaders and seeing relationships become deeper with God, and I tried to sum up our 'new team' in a simple phrase. As has happened with many before me, I ended up blurting out something God had been cultivating for a while. I said, 'Paul wants to bring people home, and I want to teach them what that means. Ultimately, I don't think Paul cares what happens when they get through the door, as long as he knows they'll be in safe hands; and I don't really mind how he gets them through the door, as long as he does it Jesus' way. We're going to tag-team our way through ministry.'

It was a light-bulb moment for me. I didn't need to be doing everything, I just needed to care enough about the whole picture to do my part, and do it as well as I was able. As a teammate, my role was to pray and support the rest as they did their part. As a result of that conversation, I have done a lot of thinking over the years about what we as a church need to be providing for those within our family, and those who aren't yet, in the light of the opportunities God wants each of his children to have access to.

We will meet people at different stages of their journey and we will have people who are transitioning too, but in its simplest format there are three opportunities we, as God's Blended Church, are called to make priorities and ideally provide for our communities.

1. **Equipping through discipleship:** teaching people what 'being at home' means and how to live in God's house.
2. **Reaching out:** bringing people home to be with God and his family.
3. **Releasing potential:** seeing people released, through God's Holy Spirit, into the fullness of the potential God created in them.

Equipping through discipleship

When we picture church, equipping through discipleship is often what we envisage first. We see a place or service on a Sunday morning that takes God's people deeper into relationship with him through teaching, worship and time together. We also know that we have discipleship groups, teaching series and other initiatives that help those who know God to get to know him better. Whether we already embody the values of Blended Church as a family or not, right now we have people of all ages in our church families who need equipping through discipleship. We can intentionally offer this opportunity when we are apart and when we are Blended together.

> Live in me. Make your home in me just as I do in you… I've loved you the way my Father has loved me. Make yourselves at home in my love. If you keep my commands, you'll remain intimately at home in my love. That's what I've done— kept my Father's commands and made myself at home in his love.
>
> JOHN 15:4, 9–10, *The Message*

This idea of teaching what makes us at home in God's house (see John 15), which is something I personally pray for at the start of every service I lead, isn't new and is probably what most of us are already doing. How we teach, what we teach and when we teach will be down to our community, and the different groups we've placed them in and, of course, what God is saying to us as a family. Knowing we want to offer this opportunity isn't about saying we don't do it at the moment; it's about keeping ourselves on track and continually asking the following questions.

- How much are we investing in this? Is it enough? Is it in balance with the other opportunities we are called to offer?
- Are we providing this opportunity for each age group, location, or other specific demographic that we are called to serve?
- How are we creating Blended opportunities to be equipped alongside each other?

Reaching out

If we are going to bring others along for the ride, we need to go out and reach them. Only a small percentage of people are looking for God and will come and find him on their own. We have members of our families who want to do it Jesus' way and go out from the building and reach others where they are, whether these others know they're lost or not. The communities that surround us are blended too. They are made up of different groups; some will be similar in age, while others will cover vast age ranges or are individual households. If we are going to reach the lost individuals we feel called to, where they are, then we are going to need to be prepared to reach their whole blended community. This is going to mean our Blended church family going out together to reach our blended communities.

> Suppose one of you had a hundred sheep and lost one. Wouldn't you leave the ninety-nine in the wilderness and go after the lost one until you found it?
> LUKE 15:4, *The Message*

As Blended church families, we need to be sending each other out. That might be on mission, in specific evangelistic projects, or it could be more fluid, as our own individual passions and callings lead. If the members of our Blended family have their home in God, then they are going to want those around them to know and live that way too. By making reaching out a priority opportunity for our church, we are saying we want to invest in everyone joining in. The type of mission I didn't want to be doing when I was younger is only a small part of the reaching out focus. We may not all be evangelists or missionaries, but we are all designed to be disciplers in some form or another. Running initiatives, courses and mission has a value, but so does being the 'sent-out ones' in the local communities. If we were all sent abroad, who would reach our home? Again, the questions the families who want to be providing this opportunity will be asking are as follows.

- How much are we investing in this? Is it enough? Is it in balance with the other opportunities we are called to offer?
- Are we providing this opportunity for each age group, location or other specific demographic that we are called to serve?
- How are we creating opportunities to reach out together as a Blended family to our blended community?

Releasing potential

Seeing people released into their full potential is an exciting thing. We all have potential still to uncover and anointing we haven't yet learnt to share, and that is why opportunities to see our individual and corporate potential released are important for building a Blended family. This means ensuring different ages and groups are encouraged to learn from each other, and it means that humility and respect are built between every member of our Blended Church. It can mean leaders stepping forward, members of our worship band starting to lead, people preaching for the first time, sharing their first testimony, or others taking on public ministry. For some people, reaching their full potential can mean helping behind the scenes, praying for others in person or in private and, in fact, it can be almost hidden.

My understanding of fulfilling our God-given potential comes from Matthew 5, where we see two different expressions of our purpose. Light is on show, visible and often obvious, and the full 'light' potential of God in those around us can be exactly like that. When it comes to training and releasing these types of gifts, we, as leaders, are likely to understand that we need plans, programmes and teaching to achieve that.

> You're here to be salt-seasoning that brings out the God-flavours of this earth... You're here to be light, bringing out the God-colours in the world.
> MATTHEW 5:13–14, *THE MESSAGE*

What happens when an area of potential is more 'salty', more hidden from view, more character- and behaviour-based? God calls us to be atmosphere changers—people who counter culture by our existence, not just by our actions. Do we have ways of increasing the opportunities for those around us to see their potential develop in these different areas?

Teaching on discipleship normally covers this, but the reason for marking it as a separate and prioritised opportunity is to show that it is equally important as a stand-alone value. Pursuing our potential in Jesus is vital to our church family. It encourages us to learn more about God and it deepens our individual maturity. Seeing people released into their God-given potential makes it a priority in its own right. We, as leaders, need to ask the following questions.

- How much are we investing in this? Is it enough? Is it in balance with the other opportunities we are called to offer?
- Are we providing this opportunity for each age group, location or other specific demographic that we are called to serve?
- How are we releasing members of our Blended family to reach their potential? And are we enabling different ages to learn to do that together?

Blurred lines and moving strategies

Our Blended Church will have elements of all these different opportunities (reaching out, equipping through discipleship and releasing potential) already and we might even find that we have lots of crossover. Sunday morning, for example, can't only fit in the equipping camp. We want those times to be welcoming to the people who we're reaching and contain opportunities for those we are releasing. Blurred lines are good. Activities that offer more than one ministry opportunity are important, but being specific about what the main purpose of a ministry, programme or event is, is important too. It's OK for our Sunday mornings to have equipping through discipleship as their main priority—it doesn't detract from what else is offered.

Having one core opportunity at the heart of any initiative

helps us, as leaders, to know where and what we're aiming for. It helps give clarity to our vision and often enables us to invite and raise up the right team. It's not that we need to create a moat around each camp that stops contamination; it's more that we need bridges in the form of people, strategies and support mechanisms that move people through the journey.

If we create a 'reaching out' opportunity, we'll have raised a team with a heart to reach, and developed a format that is welcoming and tailored to people in those first steps of faith. Now we could choose to 'warm' that group up gently. By slowly increasing the discipleship element and the exposure to more teaching, we could start to 'morph' the reaching group into an equipping one, before really heating things up and getting them preaching, leading worship and running prayer ministry for each other. We would be doing an amazing thing for those people, but at several points during the journey we would have needed team changes so that we could bring in disciplers and trainers. Or, for continuity and relationship, we might have kept the original team, but in roles that they potentially weren't as passionate about. There are many examples of this working well, but as a model of whole church ministry, of running a church that prioritises these three opportunities for all, it isn't always the best. It keeps like-minded, same-faith-stage people together and isn't conducive to becoming one Blended family. Instead of bridges for people to travel between opportunities, with increased possibility of crossover and relationship building, we'd have separate groups with borders of convenience.

If instead we create groups, times and events that have only one of these opportunities as its main value, then transfer, movement and community become vital. All Blended ministries are going to be welcoming and accepting; all groups are going to be run by those who love Jesus, and so his teaching is going to be informing foundations and values in what is happening, and all events and activities can serve as the perfect training ground for some. This approach brings our vision for being Blended right to the heart of how we provide these God-given opportunities, and that is an exciting thing.

From this perspective, being a Blended Church means being a church that actively creates opportunities for all of God's people. It's about creating a community of individuals who are moving towards God with those he has placed around them. The necessity for strategies that take those we have reached and that find room for them in discipleship will become a priority because we have a heart to give them new opportunities to build their faith. We'll find people's access to environments that further their relationship with God becomes more important, and creating those environments will excite others about being released into their God-given potential. As we focus on these distinct areas of opportunity, new ideas will occur as natural extensions of what God is doing in his people, and that will lead to ways of cementing our church family as a whole. In turn, this will move us to building, for our entire community, a family that best reflects Jesus' design for his body, as individually and corporately we journey towards him together.

As leaders, we can do more than put on church events and services. We want to build a Blended Church ministry that doesn't just do things but enables people to be proactive and participate in their own personal journey with the three opportunities: reaching out, equipping through discipleship, and releasing potential. We want our entire beautiful and Blended family to have access to all the opportunities God has for them as they pursue him. We want to construct a ministry that is open and spiritually inviting to those who don't know God at all. We want structure that enables us to learn together about God, faith and life, and we want a place to invest in people, so that, together, we grow and excel in our potential and in all that God has called us to be.

Chapter 4

Training a Blended Church

We've covered a lot about being Blended, being a whole church together and the broad brushstrokes of being God's called-out people in spirit and in structure. How do we embody these Blended values when we're apart?

We can think of being apart as having two functions: training for when we're together and enjoying our time in separate groups. What if both of those functions could become the same thing? What if the way we function when apart takes advantage of being in smaller groups, builds us up separately and trains us to blend perfectly when we're together?

Training apart to be together

There's a danger when thinking formulaically that we can end up with a massive tick list of things to achieve. We now have three sets of opportunities (reach out, disciple, release) to process, think through, collate and establish. That's a lot, by anyone's standards, and I'm not sure they are all as separate as they can sound when you read them on a piece of paper. The reason this book isn't called 'Ten Steps to Becoming Blended' is because, just like our relationship with God, our relationship with his church is more

> I am the Vine, you are the branches. When you're joined with me and I with you, the relation intimate and organic, the harvest is sure to be abundant.
> JOHN 15:5, *The Message*

intimate and organic than having a tick sheet to complete.

We don't need to separate out our Blended heart when we are planning for our separate groups. Division comes when we see being apart as fundamentally different from being together. Sharing our influences with each age group means those influences exist even when the 'others' aren't around. From the ground up, our programmes, series and services need to have the heart of being Blended. Training apart to be together isn't an add-on in a Blended Church; it's not a new initiative that will fade when the season changes. It's the guide that created the fundamental choices about who we are and how we are going to be church, from the beginning.

An example

Worship is a great example of how this plays out. If we split our church up into the 'natural age groups' that are traditionally used across the Western world, we would find ourselves with preschool, primary-aged children, secondary-aged youth and adults (although we could easily split them up further, but that doesn't regularly happen, so let's not give ourselves any more work right now). Each group has a different way of worshipping and traditionally a different set of songs and styles from the rest. For a church that is happy to be separate and may even have the conviction that this is the best way to be, then this makes sense, and, with big enough teams, is easy to accomplish. Every year, when children and youth move groups, there's a bit of relearning to do, but nothing major or disastrous. This system is serving churches well all across the world. It means handover and crossover need to be thought through well for events to run smoothly, but that is doable. However, just because it's 'working' it doesn't mean it's the right choice for everyone.

Blending our worship looks different. It means that we take the time to create a core of songs that everyone knows. It means having people meeting together from all of our age groups to have a say in creating that core 'songbook', and it means compromise from the place of a shared Blended heart.

It's a lot of effort, and can mean relearning the way we do things as a whole church family, but here's the fruit of that choice: when we come together, we all sing the same tune. We all feel comfortable and included, honoured and empowered. No longer are there kids' songs, youth songs and adult songs. No longer are there groans from the adults or bored faces on the children. There's togetherness, and that brings freedom and so much joy. The process of worship becomes about picking songs that release the heart of worship into our church family, not about suiting our style or way of doing things. If a simple song (previously labelled as kids' song) isn't spiritual or biblical enough for the adults, then should we really be singing it with the children anyway? If a song is so full of Christian jargon that it makes no contemporary sense any more, with the result that our children can't engage with it and mean what they are singing, then is it really the right song for our adults, considering there will be visitors in any given session, who we hope will meet Jesus for the first time? The aspect that discounts a song for one age range may just be the reason it doesn't fit in with our whole family either. I'm not saying we shouldn't have songs tailored to a specific age group; I just wonder if the majority of them need to be like that.

What can this look like?

Our church life and building blocks are not a tick sheet of things we need to cover; they are the ministry we're called to, split into different sections so that one by one we can examine what we do right now and reform each part (and each other) in the light of knowing Blended isn't just possible, but that it's worth it.

Training apart to be together is about being Blended at our core, and it's about knowing that when we choose to share our way of doing things with others in church, they will cherish it—so much so that it will change the way they do things fundamentally, showing that there is always space in their programme for us. It paves the way for the times when we're together, and makes the times when we're apart better too.

Sunday mornings are potentially the time we'll be pioneering Blended Church first as that's most churches' easy option for meeting altogether, so that time is a great opportunity to ponder these new ideas. Each age group represented on a Sunday morning will have its own way of 'doing church', but as the value for training apart to be together develops and grows, the way we do things apart will shift and lead us to doing things apart that contribute to how our formats and programmes work when we are together. The 'normal adult service' will look more like kids' church and vice versa. What's exciting is that it won't be because of any sense of compulsion—but because of the way we are building our church intrinsically, we will want it to change.

The format of our mornings in the kids' groups will start to reflect the adult service. We will go from themed and individual activities to running kids' church services in the same way as the talks, worship sets and ministry times of the adult congregation. It'll be a big shift from the more traditional session and lesson planning to having a repeated service structure, splitting our time each week into regular slots based on the activities of church (worship, teaching, ministry for the specific length of time appropriate for each age group) and the other building blocks referred to in chapter 7, rather than having activities that fit with the theme of the specific week. It means the workload for the team will greatly diminish, as the way we do things changes and new habits are formed. Sunday morning sessions will move from individually planned lessons to a repeatable format that enables the leader to concentrate on how God is asking them to lead, and the teacher to focus on what God is asking them to communicate—just like in 'adult church'.

This repetition of format builds good habits, takes away the need for 'original ideas' each week and creates a reassuring and predictable running order that doesn't lead to stale, boring programmes, but to a community of believers moving forward together. It will also be a great start to creating a special needs-friendly environment, with running orders young people can become familiar with and find comfort in. As adults, we often follow the same pattern each week, whether we use liturgy or not. That is something we have to teach those engaged in the kids and youth ministry, who often try to 'keep things fresh' by constantly changing their programmes.

Sunday mornings and the discipleship opportunities they contain are a great place to start the meaningful conversations between each age range, that release everyone to ask these questions: what do I have to learn from 'your way'? And how can 'my way' bless and impact you?

The way our churches look right now will be different from each other, and when we invest in becoming Blended, they will ultimately still look different (in line with God's plan for our specific community), which makes it hard to paint the picture of what 'things will look like'. However, here are some reflections on the areas of worship, teaching and formatting, and how Blended values can find their way into these age groups.

Reflections: preschool-aged children

Formatting: It's all about the atmosphere we create. The fullness of what God has to offer his children can be translated into the environment we build up. With people so young, things will be fast paced, and lines between activities will be blurred, but they will contain all the building blocks of church (more of this in chapter 7) and all of the three opportunities mentioned in chapter 3 we want for this group.

Worship: Here is where the simple 'kids' songs' will be used the most to help us grow in spirit-filled worship. The simple songs from our Blended songbook will be used too and will also help in creating the atmosphere as a constant backdrop and backing track. Those songs the children aren't singing yet become music for times of quiet and of ministry, so they'll be familiar and comfortable to all.

Teaching: The language of the Bible can feel too old for younger children but, even so, phrases like 'Holy Spirit' and 'kingdom of God' and lessons like how to pray for each other and how to tune into God still need to be in our programmes. Our teaching may end up shorter, so that our children learn, in small detail, God's big picture, while we also invest in building community with them.

Reflections: primary-aged children

Formatting: It's about taking the atmosphere the younger children will have been used to and using it to create a place for equipping each child to play a more active part in their church. By now, we will probably have more pronounced sections of our programme so that we are beginning to signpost what we're doing and drip-feeding the reasons why we're doing it. There'll be conversation and dialogue the whole time, as we let the children start to test the church that they have.

Worship: There's every chance our children won't have the stamina in worship that our older family members have, so we're going to need to grow that and build it up. Teaching on the meaning of our songs will become really important and equipping children to do things 'their way' will take time and be a process. We'll keep a few of their earlier songs but we'll use the appetite the children have for worship to teach the songs our entire family uses and enable the children to put their own stamp on them. That'll take time but it'll be worth it because the children's worship will be authentic, and they'll grow in using it as a tool to reach up to heaven, regardless of what crowd of people is around them.

Teaching: Here will be the chance for the children to learn the truths that we adults wished we had known sooner. As the adults are learning how to become free, the children will be learning what freedom looks like. When teaching about the same topics as the adults, sessions might take a bit of rewriting because the children do not have the same bad habits as the adults, and our everyday illustrations won't look like theirs. The kids will be braver too. For example, they'll find training as their own prayer ministry team much easier and be more likely to give preaching a go. As their leaders, we will want to teach them as much as we are able about the power God gives us, so that they have confidence in him, and in their calling, as early as possible.

Reflections: secondary-aged youth

Formatting: This format will come as an extension to the children's work and bridge the gap between children and adults. There's every possibility that the adults' way of doing things has been so informed by the way children and youth do things that, by now, all three groups will have the same general running order. We'll want to stretch this group more and more, taking to heart our value for growing and giving over more opportunities to them. This will, of course, lead to their way of 'doing things' changing with them, and so we'll need to find ways of feeding back and feeding in what is happening to the congregations in the other age groups.

Worship: Our teenagers will have had an amazing foundation by now, of freedom in worship and knowing the joy of it. With puberty around the corner, some are likely to become more timid and the size of the groups they're in will matter more. The occasions to stand as a bigger crowd (maybe sometimes with just the adults) will be how we give them opportunities to maintain their freedom. They'll already know the songs and be starting to teach the church some new ones that they've discovered themselves. They will understand that, in their Blended family, an open conversation, of which they know they are a part, can happen.

Teaching: Our teaching will have the potential to look like the adults' and like the children's. We'll have our own mix of things just for them too, and those topics might be picked up by the others to learn from as well. Life and temptation will be becoming more what consumes their thinking, and the opportunity to stretch and challenge them to include God in life decisions will be vital.

Reflections: adult congregation

Formatting: Our way of doing things as adults, with the different elements that our congregation feels are important, will have found its way into the children's and youth programmes. All the adults will have been open and humble enough to let the children share with them how they do things and, as leaders, we'll have been inspired to create those same opportunities for the adults. By now, the expectation of all of God's people being in leadership will have been learnt in multiple layers, and just like the youth and the children, adults will be leading and growing together as they step up and give things a go.

Worship: Adults will want to be as free as the children, as loving of the crowd as the youth, but they'll also be working out for themselves how they worship. There may be some habits they need to break, and some experimenting to do too. They will need the support of the whole church family for that. 'Their way' of doing things, as the parents (spiritual and biological) in our church family, will help the spiritual temperature of our whole Blended family increase, so, as leaders, we will want to invest in that. As each adult discovers freedom, they will be sharing that with people of all ages, praying for them, teaching them and blessing them.

Teaching: The adults will have their own programme of what God wants them to know and what he wants to do in their lives. There will be times when we want the whole of our family to be on the same teaching path, and times when the adults go their own way. It might be that we all follow the same story, the same book of the Bible or the same theme, and we'll take time to work out how that looks for each age group. The atmosphere of the youngest will filter into the atmosphere of the older generations, and the simple ways of signposting what we are doing and why, which our children need, will help us teach and lead in a way that welcomes those adults who haven't yet 'learnt' our way of doing things. As leaders, we'll be asking the question: do we really need to do things in a way that needs to be learnt first?

Having a Blended heart at the foundation of our church means starting a conversation that we never plan to finish. It means we will value how we get to where God is leading, over how soon we arrive. We can be a training church—a church that, by its nature, raises us all up to engage individually and contribute to the whole, whatever age, background and experiences we have.

Chapter 5

Growing a Blended Church

A wise friend once told me that as a church leader you don't aim for growth, you aim for health; that instead of being concerned about how many people you get through the door, you focus your attention on enabling those around you to be developing and maturing relationships with each other and with God. He was right. Of course, our evangelist side at this point wants to cry out that the more people who come in, the more hear about Jesus; while the discipleship and training parts of us are thinking, 'Yes!' There's a tension represented in my friend's statement that often leads us to forget that both health *and* growth are godly. What I think my friend was saying was that, where health is prioritised, growth happens naturally. However, when growth is prioritised, health doesn't always follow.

What is growth?

A growing church is a church that is growing together—in maturity, in depth of relationship and sometimes in numbers. Raising teams and developing leaders is how we grow as a Blended family. As leaders, our job is to help those around us to stand up, to take on the roles, responsibilities and opportunities to which God is calling them. We need to format and lead our Blended Church in a way that relies on its members of all ages. Of course, we could often do it all ourselves, and a lot of the time people would like us for it. It's non-confrontational, it's less work

> This is how much God loved the world: He gave his Son, his one and only Son. And this is why: so that no one need be destroyed; by believing in him, anyone can have a whole and lasting life.
> JOHN 3:16, *The Message*

for them and even if we were giving ourselves a sensible and manageable amount of work to do (which, let's face it, we're not known for!), that's not the point. God could have saved the world on his own, he was big enough to beat sin and death from his position in heaven, but he chose a different way—

he chose to embody humanity. Jesus could have spent his three years in ministry doing it solo, and not having to repeat himself so much, but he chose those twelve men to be a part of his mission team. Sure, they slowed him down at times, got him in trouble and caused messes he had to fix, but they were faithful, they were learning and they were growing. The exciting extension of what Jesus did for them is that they in turn taught others to be faithful, to be on that journey of discovering and learning, and they said, 'Yes!' when they were sent out to grow God's church.

Jesus called them out, and they came. They were longing for purpose, for mentoring and probably for adventure too.

> 'Come with me. I'll make a new kind of fisherman out of you. I'll show you how to catch men and women instead of perch and bass.' They didn't ask questions. They dropped their nets and followed.
> MARK 1:17–18, *The Message*

Our church families are full of people with the same longings, because that is how God made his people. There may be many layers of self-doubt, disillusionment and even bad behaviour stacked up on top of his initial design, but underneath beat the hearts of God's called-out children. It might be that no one ever thought to raise up (into leadership) members of our Blended family before they turned 18. As leaders, we need to do what Jesus did and call them out, and include every single person when we do.

One of my favourite games when growing up was pick-up sticks. I loved getting right down on the floor and slowly teasing out one stick from the pack. I honed the skill of not moving anything else as I selected and freed my chosen mark. Raising leaders in church can often look like that. Church is this delightful bunch of people, relaxed and resting, lying down in whichever way they want. Every so often, someone is plucked from the crowd, ideally without displacing anyone else, and singled out for a new job. If we imagine that those sticks are fulfilling their potential at the beginning of the game, when they are all held together, standing up, primed for a bigger, more structural role, then it's only when the individual stick is removed that it can be held again in its rightful and purposeful position. What if the format of our church family was designed to be the hands that hold everyone up straight?

Churches often have consciously let their sticks fall, out of a desire to bring freedom and take the pressure off—both important and godly desires—but there's a cost to doing it in our earthly way and not in God's way. Freedom without boundaries isn't the joy it promises to be. Instead it's often debilitating. Having a structure of total 'laid down' freedom for our families, rather than a structure that holds them up and holds them to account for their God-given purpose, isn't the model Jesus lived out. He didn't say, 'If you fancy it, why don't you pop along later?' or 'I'm going over here, there's space if you want to join in the next five minutes.' He said, 'Come!', and he absolutely expected his disciples to do so, immediately! He was scooping up those sticks and holding them tall, speaking straight to their hearts and purpose, and that has power.

Does the way we run our church services, ministries and activities encourage people to step up? Are we willing to have services that are less polished if it means that we can have someone preaching, leading and experimenting for the first time, in front of us? Letting people stay in the passive position of lying down might be part of the culture we're living in right now, but with God this can change. As leaders, we can shift our hearts and, when connected to God's power, that will shift our church families and open them up to a new way. It'll take time, it'll take effort and it'll probably take experiencing activities going off plan, but it'll be worth it. To be on the journey of building a Blended Church that relies upon and utilises every single member of its body, each standing tall in their individual calling, is what the corporate calling of Blended Church is. That freedom, that support, should be open to all of God's children, however young, whatever their background and whatever their gifting.

Being a Blended Church isn't just about our ministry being full of people of all ages. It's about delighting in the fact that we are varied in age and working to lead and grow together. As teams are raised to minister, preach and serve, and in the many other areas of ministry, we need not just to be making sure we have people *for* each 'age group' but people *of* each age group in those teams. If we believe that we, as adults, have things to learn from children, then we should be open to hearing them preach. If our kids have a value for their older peers, then why can't their groups include opportunities for adults and teenagers who are learning to preach, especially as the shorter time slot will often help those just starting out in teaching? More than that, we should be creating contexts for Blended teams who have all ages involved and who rely on all ages. The welcome team, for example, is a great place where all ages need to be represented, where each generation is placed to welcome their visitors for that morning or session.

One morning I visited a church that had just moved into their new building. I knew the kids very well and so they gave me a tour of their 'new pad'. As we went round, I learnt about which rooms they could go in, and which were worth going in anyway. I was instructed on which cupboards had toys and which fridges might have food (it was a big church!). When we got to the prayer room, they quietly checked inside before taking me in. They had real respect for the space and, when we got in and the door was closed, they squealed with excitement. 'Can we show you the best bit?' they giggled. Of course I said yes. I wondered if they were going to point out the ten-foot cross from their old church building mounted high on the wall, or the giant walls of glass that meant you could see out to their new neighbours, but I was wrong. They showed me the light switch. It was touch-sensitive and had a circle around it. They showed how, as their fingertip went around the circle, the whole room changed colour as every spotlight transitioned through the whole of the colour wheel.

Everyone deserves a tour like that, a tour specifically designed for them; to be led by other ages and see the world through their eyes. We all have the ability to lead as the gifting God has given us directs, and to be led by those of our own age and all the ages we aren't. I loved that tour. I learnt nothing about any room from the waist up (because that was how tall my tour guides were) but it didn't matter at all—I still felt at home.

The structure of team

So, if we're going to be a Blended Church that creates the kind of support that empowers and expects everyone to be standing together, does that mean we have no followers or helpers any more but only leaders, senior pastors and vicars from now on? That's a scary thought! The answer is yes and no. All of God's people are called to stand tall and bear weight, and are equipped by God to be leaders in their life, but that doesn't mean we all have a calling to be the boss. The dynamics of people and the dynamics of teams often fluctuate as people join in, become trained and are sent off. At any given point, we'll have people in our church families, and in our individual ministry areas, who are in one of these three stages or transitioning from one to the next.

The way we understand and structure our teams needs to engage with the fact that our Blended Church is growing together and in number, because, if we are becoming a supportive and releasing structure, then we'll have more evangelists in our schools, workplaces and streets, bringing the next layer of our connections into our family. Whether talking about the overall leadership structure or an individual team (for example the youth team, prayer ministry team, preaching team), there are ways of functioning within the supportive freedom that allow God's people to stand tall.

Picture a Chinese street parade. It's colourful, loud and runs straight through the middle of a community. It unites a crowd and defines a culture. As leaders, we want our church families to be doing that; to be at the centre of our community uniting everyone and redefining our culture from earthly to heavenly. For that we need to be building

God-appointed and Blended teams who are colourful and loud, who know they are a part of our community and who are working towards digesting, accepting and upholding the teaching and values of our church family.

At the heart of the Chinese parade I am picturing is the dragon—a collection of strong people all pulling in the same direction, who work together to create the display that everyone sees. They trust each other, understand each other and are the element of the parade that everything else is built around. In the same way, we need to be growing a team of key members who all trust, understand and uphold the values and dreams of our ministry, who have the character to lead and the commitment to be there for the long haul. It takes time and practice to have the connection between the individual dragon performers, before they are able for one of them to jump up and another to place their knees underneath instantaneously to create the next choreographed move, or to move fast across the street and not have the tailpiece dragging along behind in a mess of screams and ripping cloth. To build a dragon team, we need to be raising up and releasing, from within our church families, the leaders to run, shape and define our parade. If we want to be a ministry that lasts, then we need to be a team that sticks together and stays around. Having the value of including everyone, and seeing all as called to stand up, doesn't mean we don't grow core teams of people; it simply means we don't *just* have core teams of people. We can have high standards for our leaders, especially those who make up our dragons, but we need to avoid being exclusive and unwelcoming to those who aren't there yet, aren't able to give as much time or are still learning to stand tall.

In a parade, there are so many other positions and roles to fill. Around the dragon are acrobats, dancers and, of course, the crowd. In a God-appointed team, we have a place for those helpers and volunteers who can give only a bit, stay just for a while or support from the sidelines. In fact, we should be counting on them being there as much as on the dragon, because that encourages them to turn up and communicates how much we value them.

We need the people who stand alone to bring the excitement and skills they have to add into our ministry. They offer support and share their talents as they grow, and we can accept and encourage that, even if it's not right for them to be in this particular dragon or at this particular time. Maybe they can give only two sessions a term, are moving soon, or are transitioning from one dragon team to another. They may be capable of being in the dragon but their Father is not calling them to right now. They are with us as a blessing. Our ministry should be shaped by the dragon, but equally open and welcoming to opportunities to be enhanced by the surrounding performers, supporters and crowd of witnesses.

> Do you see what this means—all these pioneers who blazed the way, all these veterans cheering us on? It means we'd better get on with it.
>
> HEBREWS 12:1, *The Message*

Then there's the crowd. A parade wouldn't be worth the effort without them—those community members who are there to see what's happening and cheer on the fun. One of the most important roles of a leader is not crowd control, but crowd communication. Drawing a crowd isn't that hard to do, but keeping a crowd and slowly enabling it to become part of your team of helpers, acrobats and dragons takes work and dedication.

Church leadership, especially within kids' and youth ministry, has this horrible and historical reputation for press-ganging people into helping out, into signing people up because they didn't say no quickly enough. This, of course, is an unfair reputation for most churches to have, but the fear is still there in many. It comes from those moments we've all had as leaders, when we face not having enough people on board and panic about what will happen. The truth is, God resources his ministries, and people are his biggest resource. Going through times of not having enough members on the team, not being able to start up new ventures without more volunteers, or carrying far too much on your own, are hard seasons to be in, but that doesn't mean we should be taking just anyone with a pulse on to our teams. We should be seeking out those who are called, designed and have a heart to be with us. Otherwise we risk denying someone the time they have to give to the actual team they are designed for, because right now they are giving their time to us.

In the widest sense, God's Blended Church creates its own crowd. We're not asked by God to be every 'dragon' in every ministry our church has. We may be part of the dragon in kids' church, an occasional acrobat in the youth, and actively cheering on the other teams around us. We may be an acrobat to many ministries, while being part of the crowd for all. Everyone will stand up in the leadership role God has given them in completely different ways if we communicate and encourage well. It might even take declaring from the front that we'll do only the activities we can 'man' with people who want to be there. It might be that we need to ask God which parts of our ministry he is resourcing in the next season. It might be about asking him who we need to come alongside, who needs our attention and support in going from lying down to standing up, or what purposes God has placed on the young members of our church family and how we can nurture that from their early years. God's people will often be willing to serve wherever is needed, and that's amazing, but if we leave people in those positions of serving because it's convenient to our ministry, then, ultimately, everyone will be short-changed.

Casting vision for being a Blended family creates the language for being a cheering and purpose-filled crowd. The dragon portion of our team might be able to do it on their own, but they shouldn't. As their leaders, and as part of them, we need to be communicating the truth that there's room for more people, room for others to step up, in and out, if that is what God is talking to them about.

Training and empowering your teams

When it comes to training and empowering our teams, it's really simple. We need to give them our 'full face'. I have a friend who regularly says, 'I want to sit at your feet for a bit.' Don't tell her, but when she first said that I felt so uncomfortable! Why would anyone want to sit at my feet? If anything, I wanted the opportunity to sit at hers—to absorb all she had to pour out. It took a while for me to see that I had missed the point. Her words were honouring me, honouring what God had placed in me, and she was secure enough in what God had placed in her to forget that she had a lot to give and, instead, position herself to receive.

As leaders, we ask our teams to 'sit at our feet'—to be open to our training and absorb our way of doing things—

and that is right. It gives support, it equips and grows our team, but it's not our 'full face'. How often do we position ourselves to learn from them? To open up our way of doing things to be inspired and affected by how they work? If I sat at your feet and looked up at you, you'd see all of me. Our teams deserve the opportunity to have that view of us.

Training our team is about imparting knowledge, understanding and information. It's vital and, in this season of health and safety, safeguarding and police checks, it's also our legal responsibility. We have to do it and we should be aiming to do it well, in small chunks, through a dialogue (albeit guided sometimes) and through our relationships, and it's in regular team meetings that this works most naturally. Of course, if our teams have people of a variety of ages in them, we need to be creative as to how and when we meet.

Meeting together, outside of our ministry activities, gives opportunities to pray together, share testimonies, communicate information and share our dreams. Teams that pray together stay together, but teams that dream together fly. As leaders, we need to come to these meetings with open arms, ready to embrace what our dragon, acrobats and crowd members are carrying. Our job is to guide, intercede and be prepared (it might even be to do the planning before the meeting and to action the decisions after it) but, if we come with everything sewn up, then who are we releasing?

Our team needs to see our 'full face': our leadership and everything we have to pour out, and our readiness and positioning to receive the riches that God will pour in, through them. Our formats and planning should rely on all of God's people working with God and should be open to including the entirety of our Blended family in any ways that they are able. Our job is to protect and cover our teams, encouraging them to be brave and experimental; to trust in the way they work and help them when they need it. This might mean offering training to younger team members, who are less likely to have learnt from being on other teams before, potentially offering them more of our time, and helping them find ways of engaging with the different ages of the team they are in. Being open to having children and youth on teams previously reserved only for adults will mean making the time to coach individuals so they are able to take up these roles and not just have token 'bit parts'. Mentoring, and teaming up pairs that span generations, experiences and talents, will help the process be holistic and not just the overall leader's job.

Doing ourselves out of a job

When I was growing up, my vicar told me that a leader should always be looking to do themselves out of their job, and it's stuck with me. When I left my first full-time post, it was painful. I was so sad to be leaving and I hated that my decision (however much I knew it was God's plan) had made others sad too. I was talking to one of my key leaders during one of the 'Now I'm going, you're free!' conversations and it hit me: he really was going to be 'free' now—my staying would have stunted him. My job had become about the leaders I was leading and enabling them to lead their 'flocks', and they were ready to lead on their own. Of course, they are now in the process of raising up leaders to take their jobs themselves.

If we are going to be a growing church, then we need to be raising up leaders. This doesn't mean leaders always leave, as not everyone is called to move on, but the choices we make as leaders will define those around us. We can choose to give our jobs to others so they can stand up tall, or we can keep those jobs for ourselves. The truth is that doing ourselves out of the job we currently have doesn't discount us from God's plans; instead it frees us up to discover the next stage of the journey with God, and how he wants to use us in it.

How will we grow as a Blended Church? First by releasing and encouraging each one of its individual members to grow; second by being open to doing it together and taking the time each person needs to equip them to step up and join in.

Chapter 6

Developing a
Blended Church

A few years ago I was being prayed for, which is not that unusual for me, but it was one of those times when a stranger had offered to pray for me rather than that I had been actively pursuing a specific need. I don't know why, but that makes a difference. Somehow, when I haven't been seeking answers, God's words resonate at a different frequency in my spirit. There's an openness to God's plan in those moments that gives him access to go deeper, and he did.

Speak out what you are reimagining

In those few moments, God put into words ideas that had been floating around in me, so shapelessly that I didn't entirely understand that they were there. What God said to me that morning was simple: 'Speak out what you are reimagining.' He pointed me to Ezra 3, where the consolidation of God's people, newly reunited after exile, met together to rebuild their temple. It had been destroyed and now they were claiming it back. They were using the old

All the people boomed out hurrahs, praising God as the foundation of The Temple of God was laid. As many were noisily shouting with joy, many of the older priests, Levites, and family heads who had seen the first Temple, when they saw the foundations of this Temple laid, wept loudly for joy.
EZRA 3:11–12, *The Message*

foundations to reimagine their temple and bring back to their lives something that had been stolen.

Our churches are not destroyed; our people are not exiled; but the process of reimagining both, as Blended and beautiful, has just as much joy stored in it. As leaders, our job is to stand on the foundations of our church and reimagine, with our family, what our Blended Church can be like, and what God is calling us to be in our community. There's work to do and riches to uncover and this process isn't designed to end but to accelerate.

Don't stop

The Blended Church God is calling us to build is expansive; it's designed to take over the world! God gives us the freedom to build in different shapes, to different heights and with different expressions. The rules of construction stand—if you want to go higher, your foundations need to be deeper; if you want more windows, then you'll need stronger and more reinforced walls—but there's one thing God doesn't want our Blended teams to do and that is to stop.

God doesn't want us to finish building. The temple the Levites were building was ultimately finished, and we can't begin to understand how that would have felt, to have a spiritual home after such a tough and painful exile. That's not what God is calling us to; we don't need to finish our building project to discover our new spiritual home. What we need is to keep building, to keep training, growing, empowering and learning together. In his design for our church, God has built in a reliance on him that will keep us close and keep us wanting more.

The planner within us might find that idea hard. How is

a plan a good one if you don't plan the end? Our creativity will probably leap at the thought of never stopping, and the leader in us is torn. How can we sell a vision that isn't set?

Why don't we cast dreams instead?

Staying responsive to God's plan

Blended isn't the goal of the church; it's God's dream for his people. It's not the long-term priority or the overall aim; it's simply the mode of transport he is recommending.

Jesus left us clear instructions before he left for heaven: 'While you're journeying towards the purposes our dad has given you, take others along for the ride and teach them what I've taught you.' Becoming a beautiful Blended family isn't what we're called to do; it's what we're called to be. It's the way we'll go where God leads; it's the way we'll be refined (because all iron sharpens iron, even the new stuff), and it's the way we'll bring the largest number of people we can with us and teach them what we were first taught.

> Therefore go and make disciples of all nations, baptising them in the name of the Father and of the Son and of the Holy Spirit, and teaching them to obey everything I have commanded you.
> MATTHEW 28:19–20, NIV

God has a plan

God has plans for all our lives and all of our churches. He has set out journeys into his heart for all of his people. Those individual journeys should be the passion and focus of our Blended families, and as families we need to work out our mode of transportation together as we journey alongside each other. Like any good car, we need to be servicing our church and reimagining what's needed next.

We're human, so we're going to need to repair what gets broken and introduce new technology along the way—in line, of course, with our great and all-knowing Mechanic. God's plan is for this ethos, this way of being his Son's body, to become our nature, our outward working of his inward design. We would never presume that there'll be a day (while living on earth) when we're done, when we don't need any more help, growth or training. So why would we ever think our church would get to that point? We need to stay in tune with God as we go along, letting him inspire us in the process of reimagining his house and our family.

Part of being a continually developing Blended Church is about being a church that is open to change. We all need change, to provide for us the individual opportunities we are looking for, to step up, to grow, to be trained and to be released. As leaders, we need to be engaged with the journeys of those around us and invite the people who are being changed by their Father to have a meaningful place in our Blended family. If we, as leaders, create a place where God's freedom is prized, then we create a place where God's people have a say. Together we can keep developing and discovering God as our Father as we invest in and utilise his Blended family.

The
equipment

There are many ways we can work together,
grow as one family and pursue our Blended dreams
for church. In this section, we are going to look at
some of the skills God equips us with as leaders to
go and build, with our Blended family, the church
he wants us to be.

Chapter 7

The building blocks of Blended Church

We have probably all been told (if not by others, then by me, in chapter 1) that 'church isn't the building; it's the people' and already we've been talking through what that means and what God's purposes are. We can now say we're a Blended family, a church family, a Blended church family, with the understanding and confidence to know that the way we are as one of those titles will be unique and unlike anyone else's version of them. The ultimate aim is to look like Jesus, in our own individual family-centred way.

Having said that, God does call us to the same core values and expressions of heaven, in our individual uniqueness. The three opportunities (reaching out, equipping through discipleship and releasing potential) thought through in the previous chapters will be expressed and offered differently from family to family, but that doesn't mean they aren't held in our hearts, or found in our programmes, or fuelling our dreams. The four types of building blocks we are going to look at will work in the same way. What we build might end up looking different for each one of us but what we build with won't.

Each person, as God's child, is called to build a life centred around him. We will each look different as we do that, but fundamentally we will be aiming for the characteristics of God to be evidenced in our lives. The four building blocks we are going to look at are a summary of these aims. Each block is an element of Christian life that every person needs to build for themselves with God. As the Blended Church, we need to invest in these as well, so that everybody has access to the support, teaching and opportunities they need to build their life around their heavenly Father. Church may not be the building, but as the Blended Church we are building the structure, support and ministries that our families need to bring out the best in them and, in turn, in us, as we journey together towards God.

In my own words I am 'proactively lazy'. I will put a huge amount of time, work and effort into something in order to do it only once. Many people think I am wasting a lot of my time during my initial project. However, as time unfolds and patterns, projects and opportunities repeat, my productivity at the start leads on to the luxury of pre-planned, previously thought-through laziness—in another word: to blessing.

I have found thinking of ministry as a whole, whether that is the ministry of a whole church or the ministry to just one age range, as being like a building project. When building a house, we do all the planning first. All the drawings are complete and the people are found to do the work; we have also chosen the materials we are going to use. We, as leaders, are called to be a part of Jesus' plan to build God's church, and it can help us to think in terms of planning, team building and materials too. It is important to spend the time to break down the God-given elements of ministry that exist to make sure our building project stays on track with God's kingdom-advancing plans.

If we have the process and the construction elements thought through already, then keeping the bigger picture in mind as we build is easier. That way, our plans accurately reflect all that God is calling us to create and we can avoid trying to hold on to an internal and unwritten to-do list.

Use these descriptions of the different building blocks below as God directs you. Let the questions help you to check that you are using the fullness of what God is prompting you to use, as you build your communities and families into the shape of his church.

Cornerstones—community builders

The cornerstones of any building are marked and set out at the beginning of the project (later being laid on the foundations). They mark out the area and define the success of any building. They also take the most time as you just have to get them right. Setting out how we are going to be and grow as one united and Blended community is the same. It takes time and we need to do whatever we can to get it right. Often that means shifting our perspective on the ways we build community. Let me give you an example.

In kids' work I used to spend ages trying to fit my games with the theme of the teaching that morning. It took for ever and, to be honest, the games weren't always that good. More often than not, I would sacrifice the activity for the theme. All that effort and for what? I decided that if I truly believed in the teaching point and the way I was teaching, then I didn't need a game to 'back that up' and, if that was the case, then I could spend my time and energy on something much more important—having fun together! It's a great use of time to build community, to giggle and laugh, so that we can be known for who we are and who we love—not just for what we know. We want to be one house, and

As for me and my family, we'll worship God.
JOSHUA 24:15, *The Messag*

we want all our members to feel it. So, I threw out the themes and guidelines and started adding in elements to our morning that were simply about having fun with each other and Jesus. We were free to do the best we could and the effects were great. We spent the energy on building community and it was worth the time and effort to get it in place. Setting time aside to have fun shouldn't just be found in kids' and youth work. How do we build these opportunities into the way we are church when it's adults altogether? Sharing the peace (if we do that) is great, but is it really enough?

Creating strong cornerstones takes time. You often have to carve them first, plan where they will go and check they made it into the right place. Setting out our church family will be sensitive to where we are and how people grow best together. Here are a few ideas I like to think through regularly.

Games and team challenges: Teamwork is of course vital to building community, whether you're playing life-size 'rock, paper, scissors', or trying to lift seven Bibles off the floor with a piece of card and a paper clip. Taking time out of the 'spiritual stuff' to have fun for fun's sake is a great example to everyone of how much you value them and want to be together with them.

- Do we believe that building community is a valuable use of our time together and in our separate groups?
- How does the way we live alongside each other demonstrate that?
- Do we intentionally have fun as a Blended family, and work on building our Blended team dynamics?

Birthdays and milestones: This is often a children's work staple—celebrating the good and the bad, the annual and the one-off. Just like testimonies, we need to build in regular opportunities to share our day-to-day lives with each other and having them share theirs with us.

- Do we intentionally notice the milestones that people are reaching in our church?
- How do we celebrate the individual as part of our Blended family?
- How do we ensure that everyone feels included?

Serving together: Creating opportunities to serve each other is also really important. Whether it's handing out drinks, tidying up or another chance to 'muck in', everyone needs the opportunity to serve and be served. There's a whole chapter on team and growing together (chapter 5). Placing a specific value on serving grows our church family and community, and models the lifestyle Jesus first modelled for us.

- Do we have everyone in our family serving in at least one place?
- Does our church family value serving, and understand the joy in doing it?
- Do we have Blended teams, who delight in being Blended and enjoy the difference it makes?

Foundations—heavenly habits

If we, as Christians, boiled our lives down to our most regular activities, thoughts or actions, we would hope that, in that concentration of our lives, God would be there. The habits we get into are really important. Apart from anything else, they're really hard to get rid of once they're formed! 'Church' can be full of habit-making activities, but often, in the pursuit of mixing things up and keeping our programmes moving forward, we don't keep these as the foundations of our day-to-day ministries. We need to live ready to witness and be observed; we need heavenly habits at our centre, to anchor us and enable us to flourish in our job as witnesses. God has given us many different disciplines to teach each other which help shape and form our lives, starting with our habits.

> Be ready to speak up and tell anyone who asks why you're living the way you are, and always with the utmost courtesy. Keep a clear conscience before God so that when people throw mud at you, none of it will stick.
> 1 PETER 3:15–16, *The Message*

We, as leaders, have a great opportunity to invest in our Blended congregation's heavenly habits, which will empower their individual lives with God, as well as our church family's witness to the world. Three ways of doing this, which fit into our formats and programmes, are as follows.

Prayer: Jesus taught us to pray daily, passionately and purposefully. Everything we do should be done from a place of praying first. The way we conduct our ministries should be a witness to those around us, and prayer enables and demonstrates that happening. I don't ever want to teach without first praying and being prayed for in front of those I am teaching. We all need to model asking God publicly for the help of his Spirit. Before each service we pray as teams, and we adapt our preparations to make that happen. We've started to pray in plain sight, not at the back or in a closed room—not because we are showing off, but because we want all of what we're doing to be an opportunity for others to see and ultimately to join in.

- How do we model prayer as a church family?
- How does the way we lead our church interact with God and bring freedom and creativity into the communal and individual prayer life of our churches?
- Are we creating meaningful and effective prayer opportunities when we are Blended?

Giving: Is our church family regularly giving money? Do they understand why? Have we ensured that every member, starting with the youngest child, understands that it doesn't matter how much someone else gives; that 1p from a child's pocket money really is better than £10 from a parent, or £50 from one budget means more than £500 from another? Giving isn't just about money. It's about living your life knowing that all good things come from God. It's about having habits that set us up to be brave and bold for trusting in God's provision and protection over anything the world can offer us. Our giving also needs not to be limited to money. What else are we offering? Our time, heart, energy, life, school, work, family, future? There is so much more than money that we can regularly offer to God.

- How do we uphold and impart the value of regularly giving to God?
- How do we raise the value of offering everything to God—not just money, but our whole lives—in the way we are church together?

- How are we modelling, as a Blended family, our reliance on God's provision and blessing?

Testimonies: Telling the stories of what God has done, and will do, is really important. We all need to get into the habit of sharing the good and praying about the bad. We need to be living lives that produce the testimonies we want to be able to share. We can't make God do things, but if we pursue him with all of who we are, then we are opening up our lives to be a part of all of who he is—and he always produces stories to tell. Does the way we meet together give us time to share, to think through our week, month or year, and find God there, and to locate the evidence of what God is doing in us? As leaders, are we sharing testimonies too? To tell others about your life makes you feel vulnerable and we may want to step aside for others to do it, but we need to be willing to join in too.

- How are we teaching about living close to God? Are we building up the expectation of testimonies being shared in our church families?
- Are we making time for people to speak up and are we actively encouraging them to give things a try?
- Are we developing a range of testimony-sharing ideas and activities that encourage us to open up when we are Blended together and in our smaller groups?

Walls—discipleship

It is scary to say it, but teaching isn't our only priority, especially on a Sunday morning. There are so many layers to what we are pursuing for our church family, when it comes to meeting together, that we have to ensure our focus is not just on the learning capacity of our crowd but follow a more holistic approach of discipling each other. Setting up spiritual habits and investing in community are all important too—we need to widen our horizons when it comes to the priorities for building our churches. When teaching, my aim is not to teach the people in front of me something new every Sunday morning, but to create an atmosphere in which God's people can encounter their heavenly Father. I want everyone around me to have church in all its fullness, and encounter God in all his fullness. For this to happen, teaching is a big part, it's intentionally structured, and people in church might just learn a whole bunch of new things along the way, but that's not the end goal. In Exodus, we understand that God is passionate that we learn all about him, but he is also passionate about the whole of us and having a relationship with us. He wants to reveal that passion to us in other ways too.

> You must worship no other gods but only the Lord, for he is a God who is passionate about his relationship with you.
> EXODUS 34:14, NLT

The main structure of our 'building' will be the walls, the communal pursuit of the truth, as we, God's disciples, seek to get closer to him. Teaching, both Blended and in separate age groups, is vital to this and so is the pursuit of encountering our heavenly Father. In this section, we will be looking into these areas in greater depth but, for now, here are some questions to ponder.

Teaching about God: Investing in the journey of going deeper into God's word.

- How do we prioritise discipling God's people? Are our values and priorities for each session and format we use in line with his?
- Are we teaching what God is asking us to? Are we teaching what we feel people need to know, or what God is directing us to focus on?
- Are we discovering the ways that best help us learn together so that we take steps forward, towards God, as a Blended family too?

Encountering God: Pursuing together a meaningful, tangible and strong relationship and experience of God.

- How are we building our faith through experiencing God in person?
- How are we investing in creating safe and secure environments that enable people to 'give it a go'?
- How are we making the most of our Blended and separate opportunities to be open to God in creative and empowering ways?

Windows and doors—passion into action

No building is complete without a few holes, without places to let the light, breeze and people in. When building church, we need to factor in people arriving and leaving. It's part of the plan but there is also much more to the function of doors and windows. Traditional church buildings are famous for their beautiful stained-glass windows, and our windows and doors should be giving equally impressive beauty and joy, as they

Before I shaped you in the womb, I knew all about you. Before you saw the light of day, I had holy plans for you.
JEREMIAH 1:5, *The Message*

92

enable the whole of the horizon to be seen from within the building.

When you have your ground work done, then the sky is the limit; it's time to start building up. As a house of God we want to excel at our gifting and passions as individuals, and we want to be active examples of the foundations we have. Our church family should be about cultivating our outward expressions of faith because of the investment we are making internally in each other. Just as with habits, community and discipleship, we need to invest in the structure surrounding God's people and support each member's needs to enable them to find out who they are. A great way to do this is through taking the time and creating the opportunities to put each member's passions into action. Worship, leadership and mission are three of the keys to having enough windows for everyone. They provide more than we often make of them. We should never forget that our lives should exercise *all* of our passions and be evident in *all* of our actions.

Worship: How do you tell the God who made the heavens and the earth that you love him? I haven't found many people who can rely on just one way. Singing, dancing, actions, writing, reading, listening—there are just so many options! If we restrict our worship to praising God simply with songs then it's not just God we are cheating but ourselves too. We all know we need to vent the negative emotions, but what about the positive ones? When we worship, we should be making space to discover how we best communicate with God. Sometimes giving structure to opportunities to explore (Blended or not) is important, but so are the occasions when we provide free time and create an atmosphere that endorses experimentation. God loves us so much that he wouldn't mind if we worshipped him with only one song forever, but it's good for us as his children to make the most of all that worship has in store. Bottling up our worshipful potential isn't a good thing. The next chapter talks specifically about worship, but, first, how would you answer these questions?

- How can we release a freedom in worship that blows holes in the walls of our churches, so that we let more of God's light in?
- How to do we encourage intimacy, experimentation and authenticity in worship?
- How do we build a corporate and Blended expression of worship that supports each other's individuality?

Leadership: Releasing our potential is all about following our passion into action and, as leaders ourselves, we need to be creating opportunities for those around us to make use of their potential too. God gave Adam and Eve leadership over their lives and the animals in creation and, in infinitely different ways, he does the same for his other children. Serving is obviously a good way of starting to do this, but we need to extend this and be learning through positions of leadership too. Having the time to spot the strengths of our family members, and giving them roles within our church, is an important step to enabling each child of God to recognise the strengths and the purposes God has placed in them for his world. Chapter 6 (about church growth) considers this in more detail but, before we go any further, what is God saying to you about leadership?

- How do we continually spot the call to leadership for each member of our family? Is our family open to spotting the leadership gifts in others?
- How do we make space for more leaders and equip them as they step up?
- How do we train everyone to take up the opportunities they are called to, at any age, and ensure a Blended expression of leadership?

Mission: It's the ultimate act of passion for Jesus to step out of our comfort zone and be missional in our approach to life. This is an area that all of God's people should be passionate about—and of course we are—but is that always incorporated into the design of our church? Is there a danger that we add mission on later, or even make it a separate structure, with none of the others mentioned above as priorities? The best model for mission within our families is to look at how Jesus lived in the tension between all four of these building blocks. He wasn't stretched too thin but, instead, did everything in his Father's strength. God is missional. He has an invasion plan for the whole of the world and he is going to use us to do it. More likely, he's going to use us in the locations he has placed us in, right now.

> So Jesus explained himself at length. 'I'm telling you this straight. The Son can't independently do a thing, only what he sees the Father doing. What the Father does, the Son does. The Father loves the Son and includes him in everything he is doing.'
> JOHN 5:19–20, *The Message*

One of the biggest discoveries I made when starting to build in a Blended way was how missional it made my plans and formats. All of the ways in which we can invest in our church, with the aim of being beautiful, being Blended and being a better reflection of Jesus' body, result equally in transforming us into being as missional as him. Communicating better is missional; releasing people in the direction of leadership that God has planned for them is missional, because it sets them off on their mission with God.

- How do we share our God-given heart for his people outside our church, while investing in those inside?
- How do we live missionally as a Blended family and as individuals?
- How can we create opportunities for our Blended family to reach out to our blended community?

The structure of our church families will grow and change as its members do. By valuing these four areas of Christian life (community building, heavenly habits, discipleship and ways to put our passion for God into action) and using them to inspire the building of our Blended Church, the opportunities we want to provide (reaching out, equipping and releasing) will find a good and secure home. Whether we have read this whole chapter thinking about how we can build with these blocks only in a Sunday morning services, or only in one isolated ministry, or for the entirety of our church ministries put together, we can be equipped with these building blocks to build in God's way, and to create a house for his people to inhabit that looks like his design and not our own.

We can build foundations that set out our individual lives in a godly manner. We can invest in communities that include and celebrate each other. The walls of our building can be strong and secure through God-led teaching and encounters, and we can build a place where all of God's people reach their potential as they put their passion for him into action.

There's no end to God's kingdom advancing and no finishing point in our Christian lives, so there'll be no end as we build his Blended Church. That's why he doesn't give us a roof to build, just more and more material to invest in his design.

Chapter 8

Cultivating Blended worship

Worship can be described as many different things: a journey, a conversation, an exchange, a release, a duty, a joy. It can be understood as being needed, expected, desired, demanded. The reality is that, at different times and for different reasons, it's all of the above and so much more. God is clear about what he looks for in his worshippers—he wants us there in spirit and relating to him in truth. Worship is about the great exchange between heaven and earth, in all its God-appointed and creation-driven glory. Although its purpose is to bring God the glory due to his name, the equal and incredible truth is that it's used by God to bring freedom, intimacy and delight to his children too. The glorious paradox is that the more we make our worship about him, the more he makes it about us. The more we pour ourselves out to him, the more he pours all of heaven right back in.

> God is spirit, and his worshippers must worship in the Spirit and in truth.
> JOHN 4:24, NIV

If we are going to cultivate worship in our churches, then we need first to have worked out what we believe it to be, and what our families believe it to be. For many of us, our initial and primary gifting may not be as a worship leader, but, as ministry leaders, we all help to shape the vision and values in our families, and worship is vital to that. Whether our role is simply to support the existing set of worship leaders and teams, or to be responsible for the worship life of our church, as leaders, we are asked to engage with God's people as his worshippers and invest in how they will grow their authentic and heartfelt worship life in spirit and in truth. This takes training, as individual groups in a smaller setting, and also as the full Blended expression of our church family.

All of God's children deserve to engage with the fullness of worship. We often think that only children need help and time to learn the art of worship, but the reality is that many adults stand in our worship sessions equally lost as to how to join in with the journey they are being led through by the band or the leader. How do we worship when the song is new, contains words we don't understand or, dare I say it, has words we don't even mean? How do we worship when the music isn't our style or the surroundings put us off? All of the body of Christ struggle with these issues and yet all are asked to worship him—the one who deserves worship, in spirit and in truth, in all situations. So how do we, as leaders, boil down what worship is, what makes it important, and how do we communicate that we are called to grow, nurture and contribute to an atmosphere that is worship-driven? First we have to look at the mechanics of the 'what'.

What is worship?

Worship is about God; it's about setting aside everything to give him the glory he deserves. For us, as leaders, it's helpful to see worship as a journey our family needs to tune into God, to refocus our lives on who he is and what he's doing, and to offer all of ourselves in return.

Understanding the opportunities within worship (to tune

in, refocus and offer ourselves to God) helps us to lead and helps us to cultivate a culture of worship that is free, God-focused, and easy to join. Simply put, the journey of worship looks like this:

> Honour the Lord for the glory of his name. Worship the Lord in the splendour of his holiness.
> PSALM 29:2, NLT

1. **Planning for worship** (picking songs, explaining their meaning, teaching them to others)
2. **Preparing our hearts for worship** (enabling us to empty our hearts and heads from the 'stuff of life' so we are free to make our worship all about God)
3. **Entering into worship** (as one family, and as individual children of God, giving God the honour and being open to whatever he wants to do in us)

What makes this journey possible and accessible is that first we take the time for everyone to understand the truth of worship. We need to build up our families to know that worship is all about God. Through drip-feeding, individual conversations, repeated explanations from the front, teaching and through the way we run worship, each member should have access to the knowledge that:

- Worship is all about God, not about us
- Our worship is pleasing to God
- We can worship God in our own ways (dancing, singing, standing, drawing, signing and so on)
- What we say matters to God—he doesn't want us to sing or say what we don't understand or don't mean
- God cares more about what he can see in our hearts than what others can see on the outside

As leaders, we need to approach the worship life of our churches from the perspective of freedom. Worship is about enabling people to do things 'their way'. For example, some people (especially those with short attention spans) may choose to do actions or dance because it will help them keep focused and on track with God, as the constant changing of position is down to them and empowers them. Instead of teaching standardised actions, building up the confidence of the congregation to give creating their own actions a try is a worthwhile challenge, and for those who will happily make up their own actions, it's a way they can lead and share their gift. Encouraging each individual to sing only the words they actually mean, and encouraging the acceptance of the idea that 'if you don't understand it, you don't have to sing it' empowers us. Equally, finding time to let people ask someone to explain lyrics, and explaining them as a regular part of our preparing to worship together, puts the individual in ownership of what they are doing. If worship is a personal journey, then we need to show people that they are free to make up their own words too, changing lyrics to say what they mean or express how they are feeling. We can encourage people to substitute another person's ways of referencing God with their own; for example, 'Forever God is faithful' can easily become 'Forever you are faithful'. Of course, all of this comes from the understanding that worship is between us and God; we don't have to include others in how we're doing it as a member of the congregation, but we shouldn't be distracting others from worshipping their way either.

Worship isn't just singing and it shouldn't be about conforming. We all know that we were made in God's image. That means we were made to be in relationship, and we were made to be creative—just like our Dad. Even within corporate worship settings we can be exercising that creativity as we pursue our relationship with him.

The Blended way

All of the above is possible for people of all ages and therefore accessible to all of our Blended families. Each of these values and expressions of worship can be found in the formats and programmes in our individual groups and, with good communication, preparation and signposting, we can all journey together to the fullness of worship experience.

Planning for worship often means planning in opportunities to train everyone up. Having a worship leader and band that can prepare before a service or event is a blessing and should never be taken for granted but, even if we have these resources, there are other options. Being Blended gives new opportunities to take the roles often given to the few and put them in the hands of the congregation. In smaller groups, we can make the time to pick our songs prophetically, with everyone in the session, and this can work really well when we meet as our Blended family too. The halfway house between these two camps often works best, where several people choose one song each early enough in the service planning process for the band to have enough time to practise the songs before the morning service.

In our planning processes we can pick songs to sing to God based on what we want to say to him and, when doing this all together, it often helps if we first take the time to invest in everyone understanding what our songs mean, so that even the youngest and newest of us can make an informed choice. From this process it's then easy to move into a more prophetic planning style, where we ask God which songs he wants us to sing. Sometimes he picks songs he wants to hear, and sometimes he picks songs that contain truths that he wants us to remember. This means we sing with confidence to God about how awesome he is, knowing that this will make him smile, and have songs being sung, for example, 'because God wants us to remember he can move the mountains', 'because he is a miracle-performing God', 'because people are having a hard time and God wants them to remember he's on their side'.

Being explicit about our planning, and exposing the whole church to the process, demystifies worship and gives access to all of God's children. By being a part of the planning, the whole family can take greater ownership of their worship, and that isn't confined to the times when they have done the planning. Having been a part of the planning process previously, we find it easier to pick up the hidden purposes in other people's decisions that previously we might not have spotted. As leaders, we know all songs are picked for a reason, but does each member of our family know that too?

Dad's dumper truck

From planning for worship we move into preparing to worship. They sound like the same thing but it's not about repeating ourselves. Preparing to worship is about engaging our spirits in what we are just about to do. If worship is the opportunity for God to take his revelation and lay it on our hearts, then we first need to clear out what might get in the way. If worship is all about him, then we don't want it to be all about us, so we have to shift our heads (thinking) and our hearts (feeling). That's how the image of dad's dumper truck was created—a way of preparing ourselves for a specific time of worship, and training each other for every time we worship.

Imagination exercises are really helpful in giving everyone the opportunity to prepare their hearts. It's a way of creating a personal moment for each individual while they stand as part of the crowd, and means simply spending time signposting well what's going to happen. There are many different images you can use to prepare for worship. I have used images of corridors in which every door needs closing except the one to Jesus, breathing God in and the world out, and I'm sure there are many more actions, activities and images God has to release this in your families too. Dad's dumper truck has worked with a lot of my church family and it best explains the different stages our preparation for worship can have.

The aim is for us to clear out everything that could get in the way of our worship being all about God from our main 'life storage units': the heart and the head. The underlying premise of the process comes from the understanding that good and bad things get in the way of our worship. Trying to plan great things for the week ahead will distract us as much as fear, shame or anything else negative. Just because we need to get rid of it now doesn't mean we don't want it back after worship.

So here's what dad's dumper truck looks like when I use it in a session. Regardless of the people in front of me—a whole Blended family, just children, teens or adults—this is the model and structure I often use.

To start with, I display the image of a massive dumper truck, the kind where a tall man comes only halfway up the wheel arch, and say that God's hands are even bigger than that, even more sturdy and even more trustworthy. In fact he is so big he can hold everything all at once. Then I explain what we're going to do.

> 'So, we want our worship to be all about God and not about us. This means clearing out our head and our heart to give him space. We often store up our worries, our plans, things that make us happy, sad, scared or excited, and trying to hold on to them as we worship can often distract us from God. So we need to find somewhere to put this stuff while we focus on him.
>
> 'The safest place for all these things is in God's hands (because he is trustworthy with all of our lives). We can dump it all on him. He's big enough, and we can trust he'll give them back when we ask—he's a gentleman after all. So we are going to do that right now, just in our imagination, to get our hearts and our heads ready.'

(Quieten everyone down in whatever way helps them— close eyes, lie down, stand up. It's the action of getting quiet that matters, not how we do it.)

> 'God, thank you for being trustworthy with my heart and my head, and everything I store there. Would you help me to give you everything I am carrying, so that I can make my worship all about you.'

We've already planned our worship by this point (together in the session or beforehand as part of our leader's preparations). Songs have been picked, conversations about what the songs are saying and why they have been chosen have happened, and so now it's time to enter into worship and do it our own way.

Entering into worship will look different for each family. Some will have bands, others CDs or DVDs—there are too many ways to count. The point is that as a family (or team) you have planned and included God, as a family you have prepared, and as individuals you are ready!

After worshipping we go back to the image of the dumper truck and I remind everyone that God is good at looking after our things but that we can take them back if we want, and that sometimes in worship we choose not to take everything back. As people refocus on the image of the dumper truck and their knowledge of God and what they gave him to carry, I pray over them, 'God, thank you that everything in our hearts and our heads is safe in your hands. Help us to make wise choices about what we take back and what we leave with you.'

Dad's dumper truck or, more importantly, the ethos behind it, relies on communicating continually the true nature and purposes of worship, and building up each person's language of worship (spoken, spiritual and physical) over time. Adults have been released by using it as much as children and teenagers. Signposting what is happening makes an amazing difference to how many people join in the journey.

Going further

Worship draws us closer to God and enables us to make wiser decisions because of that closeness. The dumper truck, and other ways of preparation, are man-made images aiming at heaven and are therefore flawed. The opportunity to prepare that we're giving people is part of their training, not an achievement of the end result. For example, having given all our worries to God, we can find ourselves, minutes or months later, worrying about the same items again, and if we're not careful in the way we explain giving things to God, this idea can cause shame in those who don't leave the 'things they should' in God's hands. Because the dumper truck is a training exercise and not a theological doctrine, we can acknowledge our humanness in this godly process. Ultimately, it's OK if we take our worries back from God, not because that is what he wants, but because he'll help us give them back again when we're ready. Worship isn't about being perfect; it's about being ready and open in the moment. We choose what we take out of the dumper truck, because we are training to be closer to God. Putting a public value on what we take back from God after worship is not freeing to God's people. Someone once told me that when you put something at the foot of the cross you should leave it there, and they were absolutely right—that's why I use the image of the dumper truck rather than the cross. The image is part of our training together in a way that we can all join in: it's a reflection of humanity reaching for heaven, not reaching for a theologically accurate picture of God's perfection.

Cultivating the worship life of our church family is about engaging with our need to be trained. It means opening each other up to the different ways of worshipping, even to some that we might not like. It's about loving our family enough to let them have influence over the way we do things.

In many churches, the existence of 'kids' songs' is a point of tension. Some churches use them, some don't. Some do but only when the kids are alone. Ultimately, it is for each church to make the decision that helps their members to be trained up in worship. I personally try to use only songs that release people into worship, that engage our spirits and contain only truth. I often find the songs labelled as 'children's' don't match up to scrutiny, and so we don't use those songs. Instead, I chose to have one Blended songbook, an accurate reflection of the whole of my Blended family. Where children, teenagers and adults alike contribute to the list and enjoy its wide vastness and, where possible, each group learns all the songs, we are corporately prepared for the times when we are all together.

At the beginning of this chapter, I said we all need to be trained in how to join in with each other in worship—how to discern the journey we are being led through, how to worship when the song is new, or contains words we don't understand, or even mean, in that moment. I asked how we worship when the music isn't our style or the surroundings put us off. The answer is simple: practice. If we only ever face these challenges when we worship together, we don't give ourselves the context to talk about them in smaller groups, where often we feel safer. It also means that our Blended worship feels like the second-class citizen to our segregated worship and that won't build up our Blended heart at all.

Worship is training apart and training together and, most of all, it is accessing heaven and bringing it to earth, as we pour ourselves out to God and open ourselves to let him pour all of heaven in. Now that's a culture worth cultivating!

Chapter 9

Teaching a Blended Church

Teaching is vital to building a God-focused church for all of God's children. The 'walls' of our church, as described in chapter 7, are made of discipleship—teaching about God and encountering him. As leaders, we should be aware that our teaching feeds directly into the structure and life of the church, and therefore the lives of God's people. This often leads to those of us who are asked to teach feeling an immense pressure on what we do, say and deliver. Simply put, however, written teaching is our own way of getting on paper the good news we have been called to share.

As I have said in chapter 4, teaching, though vital, is not the only priority of church, especially in our Sunday services. It has a major structural role in our building blocks, but it is not the overall aim—the fullness of the relationship God wants to build with his children is, and that includes having space to encounter him as well as learn about him. Teaching is our human way of pointing to God through his own words, our own understanding of him and his presence, through his spirit, in and around the people we are teaching and their situations.

Teachers

In Acts, we hear about Peter and John. They were having it tough because of their relationship with Jesus, their belief

God authorised and commanded me to commission you: Go out and train everyone you meet, far and near, in this way of life, marking them by baptism in the threefold name: Father, Son, and Holy Spirit.
MATTHEW 28:18–20,
THE MESSAGE

in God and their ability to tell as many people as would listen the good news Jesus had told them to spread. We see that it was their prayers, and the team God put around them, that kept them on track with the job Jesus had given them: to spread the word of who he was, what his Dad was doing and how we should be living.

God loves us and he gives us all jobs to do, as part of his plan for the world. Some jobs are shared between all of us, and some jobs are for individuals. You could argue that teaching comes into both categories. We all have a calling to share our testimonies and to tell those around us who Jesus is, and some of us have the additional role of teacher. The point is, whether we feel it is part of our individual calling or our corporate responsibility as part of the body of Christ, we can all be empowered by God to 'proclaim good news to the poor [God's truth], bind up the broken-hearted [through God's truth], and proclaim freedom for the captives [which is God's truth]' (see Isaiah 61:1–2, NIV). Peter and John received the Holy Spirit, God's anointing, and had God's people around them to support their teaching ministry. They stood on the truth that they could do anything through Jesus and tackled each challenge with confidence. At times we may be unsure we can do it, but we know a God who can.

If your gift is serving others, serve them well. If you are a teacher, teach well.
ROMANS 12:7, NLT

God empowers his people to be who he created them to be, and he gives us each other as his resource. We all need to be willing to share what God has blessed us with and to be a part of other people's journeys.

Teaching for me has become a joy and a privilege, and it has been in the process of working out how to teach that I have seen not just my ministry, but my relationship with God grow. Many years ago, two leaders passed on their way of teaching to me, which transformed my way of doing things. They gave me a model that had only four words in it. These words have helped me feel prepared to teach and confident to speak. They have helped to unlock my ability to take God's truth and communicate it to the best of his ability (not mine), with the anointing and power of his good news. I have had the privilege of watching the poor in faith become rich, the broken-hearted healed, and the captive set free, because of what God's truth can do.

Interestingly, I don't actually know how these two leaders use these words or in fact if they still do, but here they are and here is how they unlock God's ability to teach, at least in me.

Point—Illustration—Bible—Application

Teachers, you are an incredibly gifted bunch. You will have many wonderful and creative ways of following your calling. I honour and uphold all you have done and all you will do, and I offer this to you as a guideline to get you started when you are stuck. Mess with it, change it, abuse its structure and don't leave it alone until it is completely yours! Why? Because that's exactly what I have done.

The model

I use this model in every setting. My adult sermons, kids' talks, Blended teaching and my testimony-giving always start with this. Depending on the audience, I will go into more or less detail, and cover potentially different subjects but, for me, the basis is always the same and always appropriate. The members of our Blended Church are all different and learn in a multitude of ways. For some, we need visual slides and pictures; for others, kinaesthetic ways of exploring, and even having things to do while learning. Others of us will prefer the opportunity to talk the concept through, or will need video clips to see things in action.

Often, all the ideas that don't fit in the traditional 'adult sermon' model, which is predominantly spoken, are considered as 'what children need', but that's not true. These Blended ways of teaching meet the needs of all of God's children, of any age. The reason Blended works for God's family is because God planned us individually to be 'blendable'. As we grow, our ability to conform to others grows as we learn respect for others and control of our behaviour. That doesn't mean we don't need these other ways of teaching around us, to help us learn with more ease and depth the truth God has for us to digest and accept. Adults, children and youth all learn in similar ways and all benefit from variety in teaching delivery.

This is a simple way to structure a teaching session where you can clarify your thoughts, get everything on paper and deliver a clear and well thought-through talk. With the building blocks in place, we're aiming for teaching in which we cover what we want our audience to hear—ten minutes for primary, maybe up to 15–20 minutes for teens, ten minutes for a Blended audience and more for adults. You'll know how much attention they can give you—as with everything, less is always more! This is followed by an opportunity to explore with God, in the light of his truth. We might be aiming to move into a time of ministry, encounter or worship together, when we can find practical ways of trying something out, talking about it or praying together.

With this model, we can delight in keeping things simple, as long as we're keeping things theologically correct. Simplifying teaching points can often be the hardest task. Explaining a biblical concept well isn't about diluting truth, but often we find that, in our attempt to explain a hard concept, we have fudged the truth behind it. With only four words to keep in mind, I've found I do this less and less as I teach. Just remember: this is not a technique to confine you. For those of you who, like me, hate a blank page, it's the start of your next greatest talk.

Using the model

Point: 'What I am saying'
Illustration: 'What that looks like today'
Bible: 'What God has to say about it'
Application: 'How we can use it in our day-to-day lives'

Point: Every teaching slot should have a simple and concise point. The idea behind this is that if the people in front of you—child, teen or adult—only ever remember this one sentence, they will still have learnt something valuable, something true and something life-changing.

Our teaching point should be the first item we concentrate on. We will all be asked in different ways to teach specific points. Whether we have been given a topic, a verse, a Bible study or something very vague, our priority for preaching should be to have one, simple point. We don't have to tackle the whole of a book or the entire span of someone's life. We need to think of our teaching like marathon runners think of their races. It's their steady pace that enables them to take the race one step at a time.

To encourage life-transforming change in our church members, we need to be steady and well paced. We should be choosing to teach small components, weekly, over a long time frame, rather than massive stories every week. Splitting the story of Moses into twelve components, for example, has to be better than trying to fit in everything, from birth to the Red Sea and beyond, in one week. Or Christmas? Jesus' birth has so many levels of truth in it, we could do a whole session just on the guiding star, but often we try to cover the whole story in one sitting. There is a separate note for teachers who also have the responsibility to write for others, but what I am trying to say here is this: your teaching point can never be too simple or too short.

Teaching points should be like the following:

- We are called to be a beautiful family.
- You are precious to God.
- God is trustworthy.
- God swaps our fear for his peace.

Our point should be one of the first things we define because everything else will come from it and bounce back to it. Basically, our whole talk is a set of sentences repeatedly reinforcing the same point in lots of different ways. It'll be the inspiration for our illustration, the truth within the Bible passage and the tool within our application.

It can take me a while to find the teaching point, and often I go through a couple of different wordings before I settle on my one sentence, but that's part of the process. We can have fun with language, picking different words and trying out different things, until we are happy. When it comes to it, our teaching point should be the skeleton of our session. It's worth spending more of our time on it than on anything else, so we get the finished shape we want.

How we use our teaching point in our teaching session will be individual to ourselves. Sometimes, declaring the point as our introduction will help our listeners to jump quickly into the journey with us. At times, we might not say our teaching point until the end of our talk, or during another moment of our session entirely. Often this will be because, in the process of refining our thoughts into one point, we have found something that will make a great introduction, like an illustration or a Bible passage.

I have found that my teaching point serves me in two ways. First, it keeps my teaching slot on track. It stops me veering off on to another point entirely, because if something I'm planning to say is not a way of expanding my teaching point, it gets edited out. Second, it helps me find my first and last few words when I'm standing up, teaching. I try to start or end my teaching slot with that phrase, partly because I've spent ages working on it and it deserves airing but mainly because it helps the listeners understand what's happening and why.

For me, beginning with my point can go something like this: 'Today we are going to be looking at the fact that *God swaps our fear for his peace*.'

And finishing with it might sound like this: 'So when you next feel scared, remember you can ask God to help to *swap the fear you feel for his amazing peace*.'

Illustration: Our illustration should bridge the gap between our point (which, although simple, will probably still be fairly abstract) and our listeners' lives. It should also be a demonstration of what we are talking about and use points of reference that are recognisable to those we are talking to. Illustrating your point is about transferring the abstract into something tangible, that the people listening to you can imagine, see or accept. Our greatest example of this is in Jesus' parables. He used the situations of the people around him to illustrate his point. When Jesus had a crowd of farmers, he talked about seeds; when he was in front of shepherds, he used sheep. We are firmly rooted in the time period we live in. I have a limited understanding and appreciation of Jesus' saying that, as his sheep, I am designed to know his voice and follow it, because I'm not a shepherd. For shepherds hearing that, the experience would have been utterly profound. It took research for me to discover that sheep have the inbuilt ability to distinguish between the voice of their shepherd and another human. Even at a distance they instinctively know to follow the sound of their shepherd's voice. Knowing that sheep recognise your voice was second nature to a shepherd, and they would have understood that ability was vital to their flock's survival and protection. When you know that you were designed in the same way, that you yourself have that same natural ability to hear God's voice and distinguish it from other voices around you, the illustration just makes more powerful sense.

Finding illustrations for biblical concepts takes time and imagination—two things that God has and gives to his children. God is entirely creative and he shares that gift with us. Knowing where to look is often more than half the task when finding a good illustration.

Good sources of illustrations are:

- Personal testimonies
- Fairy tales
- News stories
- Jokes and comedy
- Bible stories
- Films and TV programmes
- Science experiments and 'magic tricks'

If we have an illustration of our point that enables our audience to lift it into their own lives, then we have made a bridge from the conceptual to the actual. Using situations and events they know or understand, like the playground, home, work or church, will always be more powerful. Our illustration should have reference points that are relevant for the age group we are teaching and be tangible and quantifiable for everyone.

What illustrations we find and work well for us will be personal to our own lives. Our testimonies of God working in our lives are an incredible gift, and when I get the opportunity to share some of mine, I enjoy the honour. Giving a testimony isn't about making yourself look good but about using a small part of your life to show off God. For many teaching topics, I know the truth I'm teaching to be true because I believe the Bible, not necessarily because of my own experiences. It's then that I look wider for the source of my illustrations.

I love films. They may not be real or true, but they are a huge source of inspiration for me. What I like about using secular films in my teaching is that I am capturing a worldly story and making it testify to God. Why can't the image of Marlin crossing the vast ocean to find Nemo in the film *Finding Nemo* be used to illustrate God's passionate and persistent love for his lost children? And why can't the image of Arthur, who would become king of England thanks to a heaven-provided sword, being called Wart throughout his childhood illustrate perfectly the point that what people think of us doesn't matter compared to what God sees in us? Clint Eastwood's compassion-fuelled final act, in the film *Gran Torino*, is a powerful allegory for the cross, and *Unstoppable* is a stark reminder that Jesus doesn't just need to be attached to our lives but invited into the driving seat.

Illustrating our point with worldly images is a flawed activity in the sense that God is perfect and the world isn't, but it is vital in the process of seeing our teaching points grab hold of people's lives. We may struggle to find the perfect example as no entire film illustrates everything we may wish it to, but it can be a taster for those we are talking to of what we mean and can sometimes also illustrate why our point is worth listening to. The truth is that God's kingdom is perfect for his children (of any age) and a teaching session that enables us to see his kingdom alive and well in our world will be as perfect as his children need it to be.

An example of an illustration I have used is 'The Red Paper Clip'.

I found this story of a guy in America called Kyle who had a red paper clip and decided to see what he could swap it for. He put it on eBay and waited to see what would happen. A girl from another state said she would swap it for a fish-shaped pen she had.

Thinking it was a fair swap, the guy agreed and put the paper clip in the post. When the pen arrived, he thought he'd give it a go again and this time swapped the pen for a boy's door handle. This process went on for eleven more swaps before the national news heard about it. In that time, Kyle had swapped for cookers, snow mobiles and even a part in a Hollywood film! Then came something no one could have predicted. A local council heard about his swapping and decided to swap Kyle's film role for... a house! In the space of a year, Kyle had swapped his way from an ordinary red paper clip to a brand-new house. When I heard this story, it reminded me of how amazing God is. Kyle had something worth less than a penny but received a very expensive house. God lets us do the same, but instead of swapping us a house, he gives us something priceless: his peace. If we ask him, he will take our fear from us and give us his peace instead.

Bible: The Bible is obviously a vital part of our teaching. We should be referring directly to God's word and constantly explaining what it says about his truth, with our whole church family. I love the way God's word transmits to the very core of my being. We all know that the written word of God is powerful. As teachers, we can use it creatively to speak to the very core of God's children.

Our Bible section should be about letting God speak for himself, in his own words. As his teachers, we are given the opportunity to be his mouthpiece, but we need to give him and his words the credit. We need to be constantly pointing back to him and empowering our listeners to know they can hold God's words for themselves and read them.

There are two main ways of using God's word in our teaching. We can use the Bible as a storybook, taking the lives of the men and women we find between its pages as a source of knowledge, understanding and illustration of God's truth and good news. By retelling those stories, or by using Jesus' parables, we allow God's people to engage with a narrative that is life-changing. Enabling people to read for themselves, or to have God's word read to them, is transformative on its own but, when combining it with a concise point, relevant illustration and practical application, nothing less than the world can be changed.

Our second option is to use God's word in smaller sections or as individual verses that speak God's truth directly, with no need to dissect or explain at length. 'God is love' is a more direct version of the same truth behind the story of the cross, or Daniel in the lions' den, or of course any biblical story. Our teaching will sometimes lead us to use storylines to speak God's truth and sometimes a verse will state more clearly what we are trying to say. Of course, often we'll go for the double-barrelled approach and use both!

When we haven't been given a passage as part of our initial brief, it can be really hard to find one, and a lot of the time it's intimidating to find a verse that accurately states the truth you want to communicate, without succumbing to the temptation to rewrite one ever so slightly. Knowing something is true but struggling to find its biblical source can be a stressful part of the process, but it is important to persevere. I often use other people's knowledge, concordances or internet searches to find specific verses when I have been absolutely certain of a Godly truth but found myself struggling to know the biblical reference. It gives me pointers to which parts of the Bible to read more fully to find in writing what I know in my heart.

When I'm stuck, I use the following terms in search engines.

- Bible verses about…
- How does God help with…
- Parts of a verse: I quote the bits of a verse that I remember or the names of the characters that I think are linked with the story
- Keyword searches: there are also Bible search engines that have keyword searches you can use, but they can be awkward as you have to choose a Bible translation to search too

As teachers, we often have to fit in with a team. This might mean picking up where someone finished or following a story throughout a whole term together. Either way, we can feel confined by the teachers around us, but the truth is that being in a team releases us to do our part within the big picture, much like any job in God's kingdom does. One of the many aspects of God's word that I love is how it interacts with itself. No truth is 'stand-alone' or mentioned only once. So, in my teaching, I try to verify this, and, as teams, we can help by reinforcing truths within the big picture of our topics or terms. When the passage I am using illustrates my point, I use other verses to declare that same truth again, to quote God directly, as it were.

Often our most powerful tool, as teachers, is our opportunity to show the truth by example as well as declare it. God's word is living and breathing and the best way to show that is to live it and breathe it. If we not only speak out our teaching but live it, the effect is profoundly multiplied. If we not only speak the truth that God's word is interactive in our lives but show it, in the format and function of our teaching, then we multiply our opportunities to be heard and understood. Whenever possible, I try to use different passages and verses together, from the full width of the Bible—linking stories and letters, prophecies and parables. Showing that God is consistent throughout his word is an important part of a teacher's role.

Here's an example of using an individual verse.

Internet search: Bible verse for God gives us peace

> **In the Bible [John 14:27] Jesus tells his friends not to be upset, because he is giving them peace. Peace is a gift from heaven that doesn't take away the scary situations we face, but helps us go through it without fear. We can always trust God, however scary the situation, to help us and be there for us and knowing that gives us peace—even when the situation seems impossible. It was impossible for Kyle to buy a house with a paper clip, but his swapping made it possible. God makes the impossible possible in our lives. One of those things is swapping our fear for his peace.**

An example of using a Bible story would be as follows.

Internet search: Daniel in the lions' den, Bible passage

> **[Having told or read the story from Daniel 6] Even knowing his life was in danger, Daniel followed God's directions and prayed to him. How could**

Daniel have done that? How could he have been so brave? It was because he trusted God, he knew that God loved him and wouldn't let him be harmed. When the stone was rolled over to seal the cave, Daniel could be strong, because he knew God was stronger than any lion. When we face situations that are scary or upsetting, we don't have to pretend that things are OK; we can go to God and ask for his help. He is bigger than any problem we face and when we know that, we are able to let him take away our fear and open our hearts to receive his peace instead.

Application: Our application point has to be entirely practical, life-affirming and habit-defining, and it'll probably have a very different style from the rest of our talk. Our illustration is the link between our point and our audience's lives, and our application point should provide the tools and understanding they need to take that same point and implement it into their day-to-day life. It's great to know the truth that 'I can do everything through Christ, who gives me strength' (Philippians 4:13, NLT) and important to appreciate the ways he does so but, without guidance on how to put that truth into your life, practically and every day, it's never going to change you or make you stronger.

When I am facing a crowd of people and I'm nervous, remembering to pray to ask God to give me peace in place of the fear I am feeling helps me to accept his gift and means I can be brave because I know God is with me. This whole section is about how we, as teachers, take God's truth and put it into the hands of God's people, as a tool. The key is understanding the process needed to link people's head knowledge with their hearts, and in turn empower them to link their hearts with the heart of their heavenly Father.

We can communicate our application point in many different practical ways. We can encourage the fruit of the spirit to be more relevant to our audience's choice of lifestyle. We can suggest ways and set challenges around the opportunities faced by those we are teaching. Our testimony slot, at other points in our sessions, will help this and enable people themselves to be examples of teaching that transforms lives. The reality of God's truth is that he offers us many strategies to bring his teaching to life in our lives, so we can live daily for him. He empowers all his children with forgiveness, repentance, prayer and other life skills that we can live out.

The key to application is simplicity. If anyone is verbally given a ten-point action plan, they might remember half of it, but not for long. If they have it written down, they will remember all the points for as long as they don't lose the piece of paper. If, instead, they are given one point a week that will fit into their life for ten weeks, there is much more chance that these tips and challenges will actually be remembered and find their way into their day-to-day lives, permanently.

Ideas I use regularly for my application point:

- Ways to include prayer in situations
- Challenges to do one example of the teaching point (give someone a second chance, receive prayer ministry, write a journal, pray for healing in the playground or workplace, do what a parent says immediately)
- Team examples or testimonies

- Explanation of how we, as God's children, can understand situations from God's perspective
- Choices or consequences games

Teaching, and especially our application of it, isn't about covering ground but about digging foundations—layers and layers of the same material, uncovered and processed. There is often a pressure to equip people with the full arsenal of God's tools instantly and that can lead us to bombard them with too much. If we, as teachers, seek God and teach his truth simply and clearly, then we won't just be releasing ourselves from the sometimes overwhelming burden we feel to do 'everything'; we will be releasing God's truth into our church family's lives. This means the foundations we enable others to dig will be deep and detailed, and find their way into the patterns of their life. We can play the long game with our teaching; we don't have to cover it all in a session or even a term—God will cover it all in their lifetime.

Concluding your teaching with your application point is important because it is helpful to have it as the last point your listeners hear. For me, rounding up with an application point can look like this:

Knowing that God can swap my fear for peace helps me to remember to ask him to do so. Chatting to God when we're scared makes us feel different and starts a conversation that really will help our situation. What places or people make you scared? This week, do you think you could remember to pray when you get to the place, meet that person, or start feeling scared, and ask God to swap your fear for his peace?

The fruit of Blended teaching

Teaching is always an adventure. The best teachers are the ones who know they can teach while still on the journey themselves. We teach from our heart what God is saying to us. He then releases us to see his children build lives supported by his word and his truth. We know that this is what will lead to a changed world through those individuals he has first transformed.

There is a lot of joy to be discovered when we learn to teach our Blended church family as a whole. As we invest in going on the journey of God's word together, we are equipped together. We build up a language, not just of memories or events, but of the teaching and truth we all discovered together. When Jesus taught his parables, he left the revelation of them hanging in the air—community groups were left with the challenge of digesting what he had just said, needing to interrogate what he meant and what they needed to do about it. He spoke to communities in order to give them the challenge of working things out together. Teaching a Blended Church results in our Blended Church growing, through God's word, and developing his heart for his community. He wants to equip us for the life we are called to but he also wants to equip us as the church families within which he has placed us.

In the appendices to this book is an extra note for those teachers who have the job of organising and planning for others what to teach in our programmes and ministries.

Chapter 10

Encountering the Holy Spirit

Why explore?

Teaching isn't the only experience we as leaders can offer God's church. As part of our teaching sessions, we should be making time for everyone to explore with us, their peers and God what they have been hearing and understanding. God's word and truth has to be digested; in hearing it we often find the need to be 'debriefed' from the ramifications of it. As a Blended Church, we want to establish a culture of going to God, to ask him to debrief and digest with us, through encountering his presence and his Spirit.

The Bible itself says that it is God-breathed and, through giving time to explore his word and his Spirit, we ensure our teaching is too. Jesus himself said, 'I will talk to the Father, and he'll provide you another Friend so that you will always have someone with you' (John 14:16, *THE MESSAGE*). For me, 'encounter time' is about including God, through his Holy Spirit, in what I have been doing and talking about. It's allowing him to have his own personal touch on what we're doing. It can be loud or quiet, reflective or active, and it can be as creative as you

> There's nothing like the written Word of God for showing you the way to salvation through faith in Christ Jesus. Every part of Scripture is God-breathed and useful one way or another—showing us truth, exposing our rebellion, correcting our mistakes, training us to live God's way. Through the Word we are put together and shaped up for the tasks God has for us.
> 2 TIMOTHY 3:15–17,
> *THE MESSAGE*

want—God is! From writing prayers, responding to what has been said, to laying on hands, praying for each other, there are many ways we can help each other to explore God's teaching more deeply. There are no limits to what God can do and, therefore, we should have no limits on what we can do to encourage him to work in the lives of his children. This is our time to experiment and explore, encounter and be transformed.

Where do I start?

Planning anything like this can be daunting but we need to remember the simple truth that, although we are teachers, we're still learning too. Just like those around us, we all respond to God differently; we all have different techniques, patterns and situations that best allow God to help us to think about what our ears have heard and place it firmly within our hearts. We are all developing spiritually and constantly discovering new ways to meet with God, and explore how his truth interacts with our lives. The place to start is with ourselves—with our understanding, with our experiences and the way we engage with the truth we are teaching and learning. Being a leader is being on the same journey as those around us and letting them join us and share in what we are doing.

Knowing who the Holy Spirit is, and how we encounter him, helps us learn to explain him, teach about him and to create opportunities for others to encounter him alongside us. It's not selfish to invest in ourselves, but wise. We can teach well only what we first understand; we can lead only where we have first allowed God to lead us.

'Encounter times' are a lot of fun. They are times that

don't just build up our number of life experiences with God but are also great ways to build up our Blended community, as we all share in a new idea, technique or opportunity. We are all going to process what we hear differently, and no one idea will suit everyone. As teachers, it's our choice to use that knowledge to free us up from our own expectations of what things should look like and give something new a go.

Who is the Holy Spirit?

Before we look at what we might do to encounter God, it's worth investing in our own understanding of God and his Spirit, and equip ourselves again with God's truth. Understanding God for ourselves is important but to teach, we need to be able to process our knowledge and give it away. Here are four ways I understand and explain the Holy Spirit to people. After that, we'll look at three ways to explain how we're designed to interact with him.

God's personal touch: Think of the Trinity as the sun in our solar system. All of God's children deserve God's personal touch. God, the centre of creation, is like the sun. Everything revolves around

> He existed before anything else, and he holds all creation together.
> COLOSSIANS 1:17, NLT

him. His very presence is what holds everything else in place (like the sun's gravitational pull). From the sun two things are pushed out: light and warmth. The light from the sun enables us on earth to see, and the warmth enables us to live. God (the creator, source, Father) pushes out from himself two expressions of who he is. One is Jesus. Like light, he is the expression of God that you can see and then enables you to see (how to live, who he is, where to go). The other is the Holy Spirit, who is like the sun's warmth. It's the expression of God that brings his life, his power and his personal touch to his children.

The Holy Spirit is how God is here on earth. By his power things are created and with his power we can do amazing things. He is the personal touch of God, giving us what we need and helping us experience our Father in heaven, here on earth.

The breath of God: The image of Aslan's breath in *The Lion, the Witch and the Wardrobe* by C.S. Lewis (HarperCollins, various editions) is a powerful one. His breath brought stone to life and, through his Holy Spirit, God does the same. Whether breathing life into words that fuel our hearts, or directly into our bodies to bring joy, healing and anointing, there is something powerful about having him around.

> Then he breathed on them and said, 'Receive the Holy Spirit.'
> JOHN 20:22, NLT

Being open to the supernatural, as part of our programmes and planning, is really exciting. The Holy Spirit is for all ages. We don't get smaller doses because we are smaller, and there is no male or female version of God's Spirit. When we need God to breathe on a situation and change things, he is there, ready to answer. It doesn't mean he's at our command but it does mean he is intrinsically entwined in what we do and why we're doing it.

Our connection to God: Jesus says that we can't do anything without God and showed this through his life, by only doing what his Dad was doing. Valuing the Holy Spirit, and including him in our plans for our teaching, planning and programming, builds in time for everyone not only to stay connected to God but also to grow deeper connections through experience, healing and time.

Building a friendship takes making the time to build a connection. In John, that relationship is described as intimate and organic, desperately close and continually growing, if we let it. All gardens need a gardener and God is that for us. As leaders, we need to show, by example, a willingness to be pruned—not to keep us humble from the front, but to demonstrate how precious and in need of maintenance our connection to God is.

> I am the Vine, you are the branches. When you're joined with me and I with you, the relationship is intimate and organic, the harvest is sure to be abundant. Separated, you can't produce a thing.
> JOHN 15:5, *The Message*

A heavenly postal service: Receiving what God has for you is vital to his plan for his people. I often describe the Holy Spirit as God's postman, delivering his riches, gifts and messages, from the heart of heaven to the heart of his people. As his people, we have to understand that there are two styles of delivery God uses. Sometimes, he posts things into our lives like letters, for us to discover the next time we open the door, and at other times he waits until we're ready to sign for something bigger, including us in the process of delivery. At these times he allows us a better view of what he is working out in our lives.

As leaders, we need to make time for both styles. Quick access to the letters of God are important, and building up the trust that they are always there is key, especially for those who are new to

> He knows us far better than we know ourselves, knows our pregnant condition, and keeps us present before God. That's why we can be so sure that every detail in our lives of love for God is worked into something good.
> ROMANS 8:28, *The Message*

encountering God. We also need to teach the discipline of signing for delivery. Petition in prayer and fasting need to be included in our programmes, as well as building in time for those issues that take longer than one ministry session to be addressed. Corporately and individually encountering God blesses us in the moment but also in the discipline of our ongoing discipleship.

How do I fit with him?

For a long time, I included response times, encounter times and other ideas, without personally looking to go deeper than my previous experiences. Since then, I have changed and been exploring my own spirituality more, and that has changed my approach in leadership. Understanding my design has helped me to encourage others to do the same and so, together, we discover new levels of freedom and intimacy with our Dad.

You're a sheep—be yourself: The reality is that we are designed to hear God's voice and to engage supernaturally with him. Sheep are born with the need to rely on a shepherd for direction and protection, and they access this protection through knowing his voice. I love that image and all it points to in me—I am born with the deep need for a shepherd to help me find the life of purpose and intimacy with him for which he created me.

> 'I am the good shepherd; I know my own sheep, and they know me… They will listen to my voice, and there will be one flock with one shepherd.'
> JOHN 10:14, 16, NLT

It's a simple game of follow the leader: Jesus' life is a great example of how to lead. He took time out to speak first to his

Father, to know heaven's plans and his Father's will for his day and his ministry. I grew up with the understanding that Jesus did what he did because he was the Son of God and that, somehow, it was harder for me than for him. That's not true; Jesus had to rely on the Holy Spirit as much as I do. As God's child, I too have as much access to his power as Jesus did. When I found that out, my understanding of what Jesus was doing and showing me through the way he lived changed. He wasn't proving how powerful he was, but how I could be that powerful too.

Our confidence shouldn't come from our own ability, and our perspective on what we achieve should be firmly rooted in what God achieves through us. Jesus understood that and followed the person who had the plan—his heavenly Father. When trying to explain this to a group of teenagers, I landed on the metaphor of a mobile phone.

In the Old Testament, the Holy Spirit was around at times, and God's power was on earth at points and met with people in different ways, but it wasn't like it is now. Imagine you had a mobile phone with a battery that wasn't working properly. You could use the phone but you had to stay plugged into the mains, because your battery couldn't store the charge, which of course meant you were limited to being near the socket, but you got a good signal there, so it wasn't too bad. That's how people accessed the Holy Spirit before Jesus. They had all the power and all the function of a human joined with God, but not the full package. If they needed to move location they could, but they'd have to unplug and plug in again later, and it was down to God to reveal the location of the nearest socket.

Jesus was the first person to show us what living with a fully working battery looks like. He had the constant charge to be able to go anywhere, followed the map that showed him where he could constantly get a good signal and used all of the functions of his phone (the full potential of humanity joined with God). He teaches us that we still need to plug into God's power and stay within his signal's reach, but that we can move and go out with his power in us constantly. Our design is the same as Jesus'; there's no difference—he was just better at staying charged and getting a good signal wherever he went than we are right now, but he promised to help us improve.

Your spirituality is easier to find than you think: In his book *Messy Spirituality* Mike Yaconelli describes what it means to be spiritual. He says, 'Spirituality looks like whatever we look like when we're thinking about Jesus' (Zondervan, 2007, p. 37). If we, as leaders, can grasp that, then we can help the people around us to do the same. When I understood that what Mike Yaconelli wrote was true for me, the internal pressure I had felt for years disappeared. I know lots of different things that help me think about Jesus, and if that's all I need to live an intimate life with God (just like Jesus did), then actually I'm set! From that foundation we can all help people have that same revelation, and be free of the pressure to do things any other way than the ways God designed them to.

In this we can often only lead from the places we've been and the direction we're heading. Teaching biblical truth is different. We don't have to keep our theology limited to what we can prove but, when it comes to leading others into encounter, it's right to approach this from the point of view of sharing how God works with us, offering humbly a few suggestions and some carefully thought-through opportunities to the people around us.

Leading isn't about getting others to do what we are doing, but about creating opportunities to encounter God's Holy Spirit with others.

Chapter 11

Encountering the Holy Spirit with others

We're not the bridge

Encountering God in his fullness, through knowing him as our father, seeing him as Jesus and engaging with his Holy Spirit, is the most important and life-transforming activity we can do. As leaders, our aim is to enable the people around us to access the fullness of God with us. Encountering God, through his Holy Spirit, and allowing him to consolidate and engage us with his truth is important for all his children and he wants us, as leaders, to journey with others into this area of relationship with him. When it comes to leading these kinds of encounters, and making space for the people around us to understand who the Holy Spirit is and how we fit with him, we need to remember one simple truth: we are not the bridge between the Father and his children.

Especially when working with God's people, we can often feel the burden to bridge the gap. We see where understanding, experience or maturity have not developed and our hearts ache for the distance between those people and God to be smaller or ideally non-existent, and we can even find ourselves taking responsibility for effecting the change we want to see. It's as if there are invisible expectations hanging over us: if we explain it right, use the best music, pray in the most sincere way, organise the most spiritually sensitive event, then God and his children will be reunited. That's a lot of pressure to be under—especially when, even if we achieve these things, there's no guarantee that 'it'll work'.

The reason there's no guarantee of 'success' when leading people to encountering God is due to our expectation of what 'success' is, and what being a leader in this context means. A leader isn't someone who knows how to do everything, but someone who has chosen to rely on God so much that they would follow him anywhere, and who lets others tag along. Of course, gifting and anointing are part of the deal—but that's on God's side of the equation, not on our human side.

Take the example of Eli. The child Samuel had been a complete miracle for his mum, Hannah, and so she had dedicated him back to God. He had spent his early life serving in God's house, alongside the priest Eli. Eli had taken him in at the temple and, although we don't hear much about Samuel's early life, from what happens next we can know there was mutual trust between Eli and Samuel.

> I asked the Lord to give me this boy, and he has granted my request. Now I am giving him to the Lord, and he will belong to the Lord his whole life.
> 1 SAMUEL 1:27–28, NLT

We hear in 1 Samuel 3 how Samuel was asleep, only to be woken by God. (As an aside, we learn that he slept every night by the ark of the covenant—the manifest presence of God on earth at that time. Not bad interior design for a few hundred years BC!) There he hears God's voice, four times. The first two times he goes to his leader, Eli, assuming it's him calling, and is willing to answer, although I think it's worth factoring in some grumpy, sleepy grunts too! Twice

Eli sends Samuel away, sending him back to bed, probably with an equal amount of grunts.

It's the third time where things get interesting, when Eli finally works out what is going on and gives Samuel the heads up. You could say that Eli gave Samuel the keys to his relationship with God, that he created the perfect context for Samuel to meet God face to face

> Then Eli realised it was the Lord who was calling the boy. So he said to Samuel, 'Go and lie down again, and if someone calls again, say, "Speak, Lord, your servant is listening."'
> 1 SAMUEL 3:8–9, NLT

and led him beautifully to the place of deep and personal revelation of his Father. Or you could say he got out of the way, took himself out of the equation in order to let God be God, and he sent his child back to him.

Either way, from then on Samuel is known as 'prophetically perfect', which is a result, by anyone's book. However, I know which perspective on Eli's actions helps me the most. Eli got it right when he stepped out of the way, when he equipped Samuel with this simple phrase, which even I can remember, and left him alone with God. That I can do; that doesn't put me under pressure to be prophetically perfect or spiritually superior to those I am asked by God to lead. I'd also be lying if I didn't acknowledge that the fact Eli got it wrong twice, before he got it right, is a blessing as well, and it frees me up to experiment in my ministry and have a fair and gentle set of expectations of myself, as I, too, work out this process of encountering God alongside others. It's not just children who need us to send them back to their Father, but adults too.

Our role is to encounter God and let others be alongside us. We'll have opportunities to lead encounter times, exploration slots and probably prayer ministry as well, but our job is not to fuse God and his children back together;

our ministry will not be their bridge and they don't need it to be. Our role is to keep sending them back to God to hear for themselves what he has to say.

So how do we do that? How do we keep our high expectations on God and not on us, while teaching his children and leading them into the place of encountering his Spirit?

Culture of expectation

I have now had the honour of being a part of setting up and reimagining children's ministry in several different churches. Of course, all of these churches are still in the process of growing and developing, and many times I've wondered what I really brought to the table, other than the willingness to go where God had pointed. If I'm honest, it has not always been a precision manoeuvre; rather, I've gone mostly for the 'trial and error' approach. The things that worked stayed and the things that didn't went. What I learnt quickly was that techniques and programming get you only so far; my asset was my expectation of God. Often, as leaders, it's not what we can do that makes the difference, but who we expect God to be.

If we build our churches with the expectation of God at the centre, then we build up God's people to expect God in their lives. We can't teach them everything, but we can equip them with the environment they need to grow a teachable heart. We can't give them every possible opportunity, but we can help them grow lives that take advantage of every opportunity God gives them to follow him. In all ministry, we need to be forming the habits that grow God's people's expectations of him.

Like Jesus, we are all God's children, in whom he is well pleased. Our birthrights, therefore, come from him and this should enable us to have solid foundations in his kingdom. We have to assume that God will turn up when we call—he's our Dad and that's what dads do! We need to trust that he wants his children to hear him and engage; that he will equip us to be the signpost sending them back to him that they need. If we expect God to be God, then we can help others to expect the same.

As leaders of ministry, here are five things we need to consider and absorb into our hearts so that, with God's power, we can pass them on to the hearts of our churches too.

1. **Change our language:** We need to start giving the Holy Spirit the credit he deserves. It might take some more explaining (with younger people especially) but it's important that the Holy Spirit is part of how we explain God. For example, it is by the Holy Spirit that Jesus healed the lame and raised the dead. It is because of the Holy Spirit that we hear God and see miracles happen. We need to use terms like the kingdom of God, even with the young, because however well you use another word or phrase, you're not being accurate to the entire character of God, or the entire truth of his word. Thinking that it was Jesus who healed meant I grew up thinking I couldn't do the same. The language I had been given to understand what God was doing was flawed, and so, therefore, was my understanding. If we raise up a church that is fully engaged with the accurate explanations of what is going on, then they will see more clearly how they fit into that.

2. **Grow in understanding:** Teaching is vital. There are so many different ways of teaching about the Holy Spirit. Looking at the difference between Old Testament and New Testament; how people encountered him; how God meets with us; how Jesus relied on the Holy Spirit; missionaries and their journeys. The options are endless. As with language, we need to be willing to raise the big questions and answer them together. God describes his truth as a belt because it's placed around the core of us and protects our core strength. His truth does the same for our spirits. If we engulf ourselves in his truth then we find our strength is reinforced. Jesus could face the temptation of the devil in the desert because he knew first what God was saying. He was drawn into the desert by the Holy Spirit, but after a 40-day workout he came out full of the power of the Spirit. That's an experience every child of God needs to have.

> Then Jesus, full of the Holy Spirit, returned from the Jordan River. He was led by the Spirit in the wilderness… Then Jesus returned to Galilee, filled with the Holy Spirit's power.
> LUKE 4:1, 14, NLT

3. **Learn the rules:** We need to learn and teach each other about discernment and dispel any fears. This is what we all should know: God is a gentleman and he loves choice so much he created it—he won't take ours away. God won't scare us and he won't use us to scare others. What God says now will always match up with what God says in the Bible. When we lead others, we need to make sure they feel safe first. The Holy Spirit has a bad reputation in some places, and so do the leaders who rely on him. If our language points to a God who wants a personal relationship with his children, and our understanding backs that up, then the people around us will feel safe and open themselves up more to encountering him.

4. Live it out: We have to be willing to be honest. We can learn together and share our experiences in a continual loop of feedback and growth. As leaders, we need to be open about what we're doing, even when things haven't gone the way we're expecting. We're on the same journey as those we're leading—we need to make space for our testimonies (good and bad) too. Let's ask them to pray for us as well.

5. Experiment: Try out everything! We can't create a culture of expectation without opening ourselves up to God surprising us. Encountering God is about trusting him to be him, and understanding us being us. Everything is worth a go if you trust God when he says you can't get it wrong! Think of Eli. We don't know how many children he trained, or how long it took him to come up with this simple phrase ('Speak, Lord, your servant is listening', 1 Samuel 3:9, NLT). Did he get it right the first time? No! Did that matter to the landscape of God's plan for Samuel? Not even a little bit. Just as God has patience with us, we need to have patience with ourselves. Allowing ourselves the time to try out our ideas, modify and repeat them, doesn't just hone our own skills in leading but teaches those around us the joy of the process.

This doesn't mean we shouldn't be doing everything we can to keep people safe. Exposing people or putting them on the spot, by design or by accident, isn't the way to go but, in a church with a culture of expectation, and the understanding to engage with it, there is freedom and tolerance to try things out. Be wise with your experiments, but also be brave.

How to plan

As you step out and experiment with your own spirituality, let God show you his ideas and inspirations. Planning an activity that enables God's children to explore him seems a daunting task, but remember to ask yourself: *If I was hearing my talk for the first time, what would I need to do with God straight away?* Would we need reflection time, would we need to write or create, would we need to pray or be prayed for? Would we need to stand (shift our physical position) and respond directly to God? Would we need to use our imaginations, creativity, or talk it through?

To lead this type of exploration well, we need to find ways in which we can create an environment for our church family members that enables and encourages them to try out our way of responding and experiment alongside us. They may take time to understand or follow us; our way of engaging may not meet their needs, but it might just illuminate their relationship with God and invite an intimacy with their heavenly Father that they have never experienced before. It might not, but the way we explore next time, or the way another leader does it, may be the right way for them.

Planning to lead an opportunity to encounter God with others is the same as planning it for yourself. Be patient, grow in confidence and give yourself time to experiment.

A few ideas

God is infinitely creative. He spoke and light was created. That's pretty impressive, to say the least! So, when it comes to generating ideas for ways to encounter him, we have his creativity to rely on. Having said that, here are some of the things I have seen, enjoyed or been a part of: discussion groups, letter-writing to God, praying for each other, praying for healing, artwork (together or individually), psalm writing, music making, waiting on God, learning to hear him speak, praying for healing, interviewing church members, writing stories, drawing cartoons, memory games, worship (in all its forms), friendship bracelets for Jesus, prayer opportunities and stations, and times to meditate and soak up God's presence and word. The best place to start will always be with whatever you would do to digest your teaching. Find a way of including those around you in that!

To follow up from the teaching example in chapter 9, where we were talking about God swapping our fear for peace, we could do the following.

- Lead a prayer ministry time in which people can be prayed for in response to what scares them
- Do artwork on what peace from God looks like
- Have a discussion with peers on what is scary and what things God and we (as friends) can do to change it (for example, The dark—God: bring light, us: pray; Bullies at school—God: protect, us: tell someone)
- Wait on God as we ask him to talk to us about our fears and to show us how he's taking them away and replacing them with peace

Chapter 12

Two disasters and one success

Encountering the Holy Spirit alongside others is a brave and exciting adventure to go on. There are so many different routes and skills we could use and, with God, they're all good. As always, we can play the long game and enjoy the ride, trying out different things at different times. The key, as with the illustration, Bible and application parts of our teaching sessions, is to keep returning to our teaching point. If our exploration goes off on a tangent, then we aren't enabling our teaching to be reinforced.

It's time to share

As I have already said, as leaders, when approaching experimentations we have to be willing to put ourselves in the path of disaster but in that challenge is the truth that God can turn the biggest disaster into the greatest experiment and life moment. With that in mind, it wouldn't be fair of me not to share a couple of disaster stories of my own, and how God turned them for his glory!

> And we know that God causes everything to work together for the good of those who love God and are called according to his purpose for them.
> ROMANS 8:28, NLT

Disastrous leading

The first time I led an encounter time on my own, I was terrified. I had led many times before, under the covering of other people. For this particular teaching session, I wanted to focus on and explore the truth that God talks and we have the ability to listen, and I hadn't done that on my own before. I started by describing briefly some of the ways God speaks and then got everyone to lie down on the floor. I put quiet music on and I prayed over everyone that, by his Holy Spirit, God would come and talk to us. Then came two of the scariest minutes of my life. We waited. After what felt like the rest of my life, I sat up, faded the music and thanked God publicly for speaking. I then gathered the children around me and asked if anyone had heard anything.

Silence. Not a word. Panic began to rise up in me and I felt like an idiot. I asked if anyone had trusted that God had been in the room and several children said yes, and I explained why God uses our 'thinking brains' to know when he's around and that in itself is a gift. But, if I'm honest, I was gutted—it didn't look like this when others did it!

The thing was, I had really felt God. I was so sure he was doing something, so in a last-ditch attempt I said, almost hopelessly, 'What about feeling—anyone feel anything?— Then quietly an eight-year-old boy said (with a slight look of alarm on his face), 'I felt bubbly.'

All of a sudden the atmosphere changed and many of the kids piped up with feelings, pictures and words God had given them. Relief flooded my body and I felt so honoured to be there, in that moment, as children interacted with their heavenly Father in a new way. I was humbled by the children and their openness to God—even if, with my first question, I had limited their responses. I was able, in that moment, to help the children see that every one of their experiences happened out of the deep love their Father has for his children, and watched as he started us all off on a journey into knowing him more.

In ministry, we often put off doing things out of a misplaced concern that not everyone will have a positive experience of that ministry. We censor ourselves in order to be 'loving' but what we actually do is short-change God and his children. Meeting with God is an individual experience and a gift we have to practise. It's OK not to have an earth-shattering experience of God every time we go exploring with him, especially if, in our brain, we have known he is in the room and can help others come to that understanding too. On that particular morning, everyone was able to raise a hand to knowing intellectually that God was in the room by the end of the session, even if other parts of their creativity or personality didn't recognise him. Asking this new question ('Did you know—emotionally, spiritually or intellectually—that God was in the room?') can take the pressure off us and realign our expectation of each other. We all have to choose to believe that God is in the room with us, while cultivating high expectations of our heavenly Father and, sometimes, in the shuffle of life, we place the high expectations on our shoulders rather than on God's. If we create an atmosphere of trust, communication and experimentation, then this will rub off on our churches.

Disastrous planning

In a previous job as children's pastor I used to get given one Quiet Day a month. These terrified me! For years, I avoided them, in favour of planning and seeking God for 'my children'. However, the more I understood my spirituality, the more I realised that avoiding these times was short-changing God and me. The previous month, I had been given the prophetic picture of a child holding a dove close to her face. It was a famous early painting by Picasso and my research had told me it was in the National Gallery in London. I worked out that the train and tube times would happily fill a lot of my day and was relieved that the 'quiet' bit wouldn't have to be too long, so I decided this made a good plan. I would go and sit in front of that painting and see what happened.

After a great morning of listening to podcasts and travelling, I got to Trafalgar Square and went into the gallery. I walked around for about an hour trying to find the painting. Had I got the artist wrong? Did I have the wrong time period? Eventually, I asked an attendant and he told me that the painting had gone into storage the week before. Deflated and confused, I left the gallery and sat on the stone benches in front of the monument, between two sets of tourists, closed my eyes and sank internally—goodness knows what they thought of me! How could I have got it so wrong? Planning this day hadn't felt like a cop-out, when I factored in an epiphany in front of this picture, and now I felt like a spiritual fraud on a day trip to London. At that moment my choices were limited: burst into tears (the looming favourite as my heart continued to sink), or something else. I went for the second, put my headphones back in my ears and played the first worship album I found.

Music is a way that I know helps me think about Jesus; I had learnt that was one of my shortcuts to God and so I gave it a go. Instantly peace filled me and I didn't feel like a fraud any more—just a daughter. I don't know how many minutes or songs passed by, maybe very few in reality, but enough for me to feel I wasn't rushing away when I opened my eyes.

I looked at the scene in front of me: people milling around, taking photos, the lack of pigeons (wasn't this place meant to be full of them?), and I found my eyes focused in, supernaturally I believe, on a little girl playing on one of the big lion statues. She was having a great time, jumping, balancing, exploring and smiling, and all of a sudden I felt God say, 'Can't we do that?' Why couldn't I just play around with God, with whatever was in front of me? I took a picture on my phone of what I saw and gave it a caption in my notebook. With no other ideas, I decided to go and see what other images and captions I could find. Over the period of three or four hours I had walked all over the centre of London and had collected many photos and captions. Some spoke of that day and that moment, some were for my ministry, and some have profoundly changed the direction of my life with God.

My plans were a disaster. Not one thing I had expected happened or worked out, but God did something amazing anyway. I discovered a new way of expressing my spirituality that has unlocked in me a creative freedom I had never experienced before. I regularly take time now to find images (the internet is great for this) and take photos to which I can give captions. My disaster was God's triumph.

Heavenly Sleeping Lions

Based on all that I have said, it would be wrong of me to leave you with lots of different ideas to try out and perfect. The beauty of your leadership is you, and I don't want to detract from that. However, I will share with you one activity God gave me that has blessed me, the children I work with and the adult congregations I have taught this to.

Here's how to play this game.

Have you ever played Sleeping Lions with three-year-olds? They are hilarious. They get so excited! They giggle and wriggle and can't contain themselves. Why? Because they expect something to happen when you play with them! They absolutely expect you to walk around them while they lie there; they expect you to touch them, to put a hand on their shoulder or to give them a tickle. They expect you to talk to them and whisper in their ear. They expect to have so much fun that they will want to play again.

We are going to do the same thing. We are going to lie down, quieten our hearts and expect God to turn up. We are going to expect him to walk around us, to talk to us, to touch our lives and even our bodies. We are going to let him whisper into our lives everything he wants us to hear from him. He might paint a picture in our imagination or let our ears or hearts hear his words. He might remind us of something that has already happened, or he might help our brain to know he is in the room.

Fancy giving it a go?

Let's lie down and see what God wants to do today.

'God, we are excited that you are here and we trust you. Come and speak to us. Draw pictures with us, whisper words and use our memories. We are open to what you want to do today. We invite you to come and play heavenly Sleeping Lions with us.'

It's such a simple game, and explaining how a tiny child plays it takes away the pressure to get it 'right' somehow. It brings the ability needed down to zero and includes everyone. Of course, you don't have to play this lying on the floor, although with kids, and when there's enough space, it can be helpful. I've done it with whole congregations sitting or a mixture of the two. It's good to explain that it is important that we are expecting God to speak to us, and that it is up to God and not up to us how he does so. I always finish by sharing that this is how I fall asleep every night. Sometimes that means I have amazing God-dreams, sometimes I just sleep and most of the time I fall asleep in the middle of playing the game. The point is it's a game I can play with my Dad every day and it has become a foundational habit in the process of hearing God speak, for many more than just me.

Why don't you try it yourself, and teach it to someone else? Or, even better, ask God to teach you a game of your very own!

Chapter 13

Beginning to build

Building a Blended Church, or a Blended ministry within a church, is like constructing a microcosm of heaven on earth. It takes time, strategy, patience and, most of all, God's power. Investing in the different values our Blended Church has (reaching out, equipping through discipleship and releasing potential) takes a willingness to rethink and often reprioritise our church plans. Wanting to construct a Blended Church that uses all four of the building blocks each member of our church needs in their own life (building community, establishing heavenly habits, access to discipleship, and opportunities to put their passions into action) takes thinking through and intentional strategy. Trying to hold on to all of these for any period of time can be tough, especially at the beginning of building a Blended Church. Here is one way we can get down on paper what we already have, identify what we still need to think through, and start to build the strategies we need in order to construct the Blended Church God has designed us to be.

Gaps in our net

Jesus clearly demonstrated to his twelve team members that to become a follower of his Dad you need to learn to fish. There are two general forms of fishing.

'Come with me. I'll make a new kind of fisherman out of you. I'll show you how to catch men and women instead of perch and bass.'
MATTHEW 4:19, *The Message*

You can fish with rods or with nets. I'm not an expert, but I am sure there are times and situations when one option wins out over the other. When it comes to the ministry of the church, we need to think big. Individuals catch individuals, but we want to be families that catch families! I don't know if you've ever seen the set-up needed to catch whole shoals of fish from the shore, or a large ocean net, but they are vast—and they mean business!

A healthy Blended Church is a church that has a well-constructed net, with each of the building blocks utilised to their heavenly fullness. When processing the question 'Are we doing that?', it helps to map out everything we want to do, and fill in everything we are currently doing. From there we can start to pray through the gaps, what God is asking us to do about them and the strategies we need to develop.

When doing this, there are the two types of net I draw for myself.

Net One: Are we offering all the opportunities we want to offer?

Listed below are all the opportunities I want my ministry (microcosm of heaven on earth) to offer to my community, as my column headings, and every age range or community demographic I want to consider, down the side. This net works best when you are considering a ministry as a whole. For example, if we were looking at the ministries our current church invests in and runs, in the column down the side we could split the church into the different age groups we have, to provide smaller group settings. We consider each age group individually, and also the ministry we offer for each one when we are all Blended together.

Thinking about the whole of my community, my net might look like this.

NET ONE	Reaching out	Moving strategy*	Equipping through discipleship	Moving strategy*	Releasing potential
Under 3s					
Nursery					
Primary school					
Secondary school					
Adults: single					
Adults: married					
Adults: over 60					
Blended Community					

*extra columns for those ideas and strategies specifically designed to move people on in their journey into greater encounters with God (and his Blended Church)

This net helps me map what we are doing and where we have gaps to fill. It means I can clearly see what to be dreaming and chatting about next, and where I can invest more of my time asking God what he might want me to do next. On it, I write what does exist, what might exist and what I dream will one day exist, in all its colour-coded glory.

Net Two: Does every ministry opportunity build in times and places for everyone to learn and grow in their Christian life?

This net is about tracking how well we are building the blocks needed to support everyone's Christian life. It's a way of seeing where the building blocks are evident in the ministry/church as a whole. This one helps me think through how I'm building. I might put the age groups down the side again, so that I can see how we're providing these elements across an age range over the course of our ministry, or I might go instead for specific groups or ministries, as below, so I can see clearly how they are being built up.

NET TWO	Foundations Prayer, giving, testimonies	Cornerstones Games, milestones, serving	Walls Teaching, ministry	Windows Worship, leadership, mission
Mid-week discipleship group				
Kids' church service				
Adult church service				
Blended Church service				
Blended outreach event				
Blended leadership programme				

Casting vision

However we are discovering and noting down what God is saying to us, our first priority is to find ways of communicating well with our team and our church family what we are doing, why we are doing it and what we think we should be doing next. For those of us who are not the overall church leader, this will be an even more important process to be starting with, as we aim to be dreaming and building church as part of the team God has placed us within. Those of us who are the most senior leader will need to make this a priority too, as we need our teams to be excited about what excites us and able to engage with what God is saying to us. Our church is likely already to have 'ministry blueprints', so communicating well what we think and what God is saying to us best ensures we all stay on the same page, with the same God-given blueprint for our Blended Church.

Building up the language we use to share is important. Not everyone will be able to see what we see, so how will we involve them in the planning, praying, processing and the building of church, without first taking the time to include them? Casting our vision is like casting a net or using a fishing rod. Sometimes we'll want to be as targeted as going one by one, and as specific as using different types of 'bait' for different types of people. That doesn't mean bribing people to jump on board! Other times we will want to share with whole groups of people all at once.

Raising a building team

After communicating the vision, we need to start to gather around us those who share our vision and are willing to get involved. For us to be able to find the people who God is calling to build with us, our communication needs to be clear.

> The heads of the families of Judah and Benjamin, along with the priests and Levites—everyone, in fact, God prodded—set out to build The Temple of God in Jerusalem. Their neighbours rallied behind them enthusiastically with silver, gold, tools, pack animals, expensive gifts, and, over and above these, Freewill-Offerings.
>
> EZRA 1:5–6, *The Message*

Including others in planning, which could mean going through those nets together, or could involve the later stages of planning, can be hard for leaders. We have so many ideas and dreams that we want to see happen, and we know that God has made us the leader in this place for a reason. In Ezra, we see that thousands of people came together to rebuild the temple; they achieved one cohesive building, and they did it together. We need to trust that the God who coordinated their building project will coordinate ours too.

As leaders, we often think about the whole, but in raising a Blended building team it can help to think instead about who can champion each individual part. This means we can keep the whole on track while others pioneer the smaller sections of ministry. The traditional route is to go for different people for different age groups, but this won't help us be Blended. Yes, different ages need different skills and understanding at times, but bringing together a team of teachers to invest in the entire landscape of our church family or ministry will bring a Blended unity naturally and in such a way that the Blended values will not need to be retrofitted. Worship, mission and building community all benefit from that approach.

Giving your blessing

We are all designed to be people who reach our potential and who exist in the spiritual freedom Jesus won, so that we can live life to his fullest. As we lead our building teams, as we approach ministry as cohesive and coherent microcosms of

> A thief comes to steal and kill and destroy, but I came to give life—life in all its fullness.
> JOHN 10:10, NCV

heaven here on earth, we need to release our blessing and our 'permission'. To each of our teams and family members we need to communicate that they have the freedom to do things 'their way' within the body of our church, as they uphold the values of the family.

Building a Blended Church means building in a Blended way: encouraging all ages to be involved, investing in a ministry that accepts and encourages everyone, at whatever point they are on their journey towards God, actively trusting that heaven and earth are designed to be Blended.

The
call

We know that God calls his people to go to the ends
of the earth, so let's go and do it! He wants us to reach
those who haven't yet been found, and to pray: 'Your
kingdom come, God; may your ways of doing things
be established on earth, in the fullness that exists
in heaven.'

Chapter 14

Being more than the sum of our parts

Bringing heaven to earth

From the age of three all I wanted was to be a mum. That's no secret—all my life I have been telling everyone. What I didn't tell them, however, was that I had a second, secret wish for my future.

I wanted to be the next Mary.

You see, in my child-like understanding, I knew Jesus was coming again and I wanted to have him on earth with me. So I had adopted the 'if it's not broke don't fix it' approach to theology and, as his first method of arrival was still being celebrated, why wouldn't he come that way again? I wanted Mary's job next; I wanted to be a part of bringing Jesus back to earth.

It turns out, I now understand, that for most of my childhood I had been petitioning my Father for heaven to come to earth. I know now that Jesus is going to return in a different way—no more stables for him—but that doesn't mean my heart for Jesus' kingdom to be on earth with me, to see his church transformed into a more accurate representation of his supernatural glory, is ungodly or impossible.

What about you? What part of heaven's coming to earth is God calling you to? We can all be the next Mary. We can carry the Spirit of God in us and allow him to work through us to continue his kingdom advancing on earth and existing as it does in heaven. Being more than the sum of our parts as whole Blended Church families is going to take all of us bringing heaven to earth in the ways God has designed us to. When God's kingdom gets added to our united body, we become more than the number of body parts we represent—we become more than the earthly sum of us and instead become the heavenly equation for change and transformation.

A reminder from the beginning

You've heard this story before, but it was a good place to start and I think an equally good place to end:

On the first night of a conference, several years ago now, a woman walked up to me and said, 'God says, "You are called to something beautiful." I don't know what that means but I hope you do.'

It was a month before the full revelation of those six words hit my heart. God's church is beautiful and, as a lover of it, my calling is to be part of the process of making it, keeping it, and encouraging it to be beautiful.

My hope is that, through the pages of this book, you hear God's voice whisper into your ears, 'You are called to something beautiful.' And my hope is that, as you meditate on those words, God's revelation hits your heart and filters into your ministry, as you go out and build the families, and ultimately the Blended Churches, he is calling you to.

A prayer

God, you love us. You think we're worth dying for and, even though we messed things up, you sent our big brother Jesus to save us.

Thank you that you made us to be in families. Thank you that you trust and equip us to be your eyes and ears, hands and feet on this earth. And thank you that when you designed earth, you made it to blend with heaven.

Dad, would you bless us with a relationship so intimate and organic that we know you're keeping us close. Would you remind us daily that your face is turned towards us and smiling. And, as you send us out with your plans and purposes, would you send your glory with us, and your peace surrounding us. Amen

The Lord bless you and keep you; the Lord make his face shine on you and be gracious to you; the Lord turn his face towards you and give you peace.
NUMBERS 6:24–26, NIV

Appendices

As an added extra I have two more thoughts for you.

For those who need to find ways of communicating a whole term's worth of teaching plans to a team of teachers, here are some of the things I think about when trying to share the teaching God has asked me to put in place for a team. Often the specifics of teaching over a term are broken down and itemised more in the kids' and youth work settings of church ministry but, if those of us planning for our adult congregations start to blend our ways with this, we will be creating an even better system, one that will lead to a completely blendable teaching set-up for those appointed to teach our whole Blended family, and give even better foundations to our Blended church family for the times when we meet together.

For those of you who have read the book and don't quite know what God is asking you to do next, I have written a set of questions. This doesn't cover the whole book or all of its ideas but takes some of the main themes and concepts, and frames them in the shape of a set of questions. It might be a useful set of discussion starters with your team; it might be a way of getting your own thoughts on paper, or it might simply remind you which bits you wanted to go back and read again. Whatever your journey into a Blended future, I hope it serves as a blessing and helpful support as you step out.

An extra note to those writing teaching plans

As leaders, the ability to condense our ideas into something manageable for our teams, in a way that inspires them to add their own understanding, is quite a skill to maintain! Understanding the way we want our teaching in each session to end up helps us when trying to write our plans down for others. Our aim is not to write a talk for each week but to enable our leaders and teachers to write their own. There is a fine line between providing enough detail to equip each teacher in our team and provide a good understanding of the direction we want to head, and providing too much, so that they only need to use the material we have provided, without making it their own. When we get the balance wrong, it can result in teachers either going off topic, or not taking the opportunity to generate their own teaching with God. Our heart, as teachers, has to be in the tension between those two realities. We have to equip our leaders and volunteers, while expecting and enabling them to rely on their God-given authority to teach. The key is not control, but freedom and releasing communication.

What's the aim?

I have come to a place where I don't want to write out a full curriculum for my team simply to deliver. I believe that to empower them fully, I need to give them the opportunity to partner directly with God and fill out the bare bones of my plan with him. This means that instead of giving them a full curriculum, I give them only enough to build up their confidence in themselves. I want them to know where I think they should go, but also that they can follow God's lead in their own right.

Obviously, training is vital for this approach. Writing training resources, 'cheat sheets' and 'how to keep on track' sheets is vital. Instead of writing reams of material that weighs down our teams and stunts their reliance on personal revelation from God, we can keep our teaching materials short and succinct and, instead, have a 'how to use me' guide. On top of this, we can write a vision for the term or topic in question, referring to the big picture to which each teaching session is contributing and release our team to add their own contributions and changes to their sessions.

As leaders and teachers, we have to understand the destination in which we are expecting our team to travel, and we need to put in the time, training and resourcing to enable our leaders to get there with us. As our ministry to God's people grows, our ministry to leaders has to increase. If we spend time enabling our teams to access and understand their anointing, we will see growth beyond our own limits, because we have gone beyond our own limits and encouraged our leaders to access for themselves our limitless God.

When writing for others, I try to keep in my head (and heart) that I can offer to God (and my team) only my best efforts. When I speak, light is not created, unlike when my Father speaks, and so I trust his superior creativity will transform my efforts to the glory his word demands. The best way to explain to you how I write material is to share some. So here is the leaders' blurb and the first two sessions of a twelve-session teaching series on Moses, which I wrote for my kids' church team.

Teaching material example

This material was given to all leaders, whether they were teaching or not, in our kids' church team. Kids' church in this context is for children aged five to eleven, happens alongside the adult service three Sundays a month and has the priority of 'equipping through discipleship'. The building block we are focusing on is discipleship, while the other blocks (community building, heavenly habit forming, and passion into action) happen as part of the format surrounding the teaching section of the programme.

Walking the way Moses did (Exodus 2:15–21)

'His sheep follow him because they know his voice' (John 10:4, NIV).

'My sheep listen to my voice; I know them and they follow me' (John 10:27).

God's desire is that we, as his sheep, know his voice. He wants to cultivate relationships with us that not only transform us but change the world! This term we are following the story of Moses because we want each of our young people to grow in their relationships with God and learn from one of his most trusted sheep.

Moses was not perfect. He wasn't the brightest, prettiest or bravest. In fact, he was a murderer, coward and general outcast. Yet God, in his wisdom, hand-picked Moses to have a relationship with him that not only transformed Moses, but also changed the course of history.

This term, we don't want to learn just the story of Moses' life, but we also want to learn from the way he got to know God and how he learnt to follow him anywhere. By looking at the relationship Moses had with God, the way they walked side by side through the good, the bad and the ugly, my prayer is that we, as his sheep, will learn to hear his voice; that as we examine how Moses got to know, lived alongside and worked with God, we will start to enable our young people to develop their relationship with God. We want them to know they belong to God, and we want them to hear his voice so they can follow him into the future he has waiting for them.

I believe the key to Moses' relationship with God was through his experiences of him. He saw him, heard him, felt him. Moses had a tangible God to believe in and follow. We have that too. Sometimes it takes a bit of practice, learning to hear, see and feel our almighty God, but he is the same yesterday, today and forever. And if Moses can do it, so can we!

As we teach this new series, let's try to focus on enabling our young people to discover their God in new (and old) ways. Let's give them the knowledge of their heavenly Father, but let's also enable them to experience him with all their senses.

Session 1 of 12

Point: God is with you, even when you don't know him.

Illustration: Exodus 2:1–15, Moses' life before he met God

From a baby, in danger of being murdered, to floating downstream, to ending up in the arms of Pharaoh's daughter, Moses was born into quite an exciting adventure! It's easy for us to see how God protected and guided Moses' early life. Moses was a baby, he didn't know God and, until much later, he didn't even know where he had really come from. You could say he had been lost and he certainly wasn't brought up knowing God. That didn't matter to God, though—he was watching and working through everything that happened.

Bible: Psalm 139:1–3 (www.fathersloveletter.com, © 1999 Father Heart Communications): You may not know me, but I know everything about you. I know when you sit down and when you rise up. I am familiar with all your ways.

God knows us! He knows everything we think, everything we do/have done, he has always been there and will always be there. Moses didn't meet God until he was an adult, but that didn't mean God didn't get involved in his life. He guided the basket to the palace; he made sure there were people to find him; and he softened Pharaoh's heart so Moses could grow up in his palace. Every step that Moses took was in the right direction, because God was watching, protecting and waiting for him.

Application: It didn't matter that Moses didn't know God; what mattered was that God knew Moses. It's the same with us. Whether we forget to involve God in our life, or haven't made a decision about him yet, God loves us and is there to help and protect us. But how much better would Moses' life have been if he had known God was with him from the beginning? What difference does knowing God make in your life? How can you involve him in what you are doing this week, now that you know he's there?

Ministry: How would you naturally respond to God's message? How can you enable the children to join you and respond in that way too?

Session 2 of 12

Point: There is no sin bad enough to stop God loving us.

Illustration: Exodus 2:11–23, Growing up in Egypt and making a big mistake

Compared with the rest of the Hebrews, Moses had a great start in life. Growing up in the palace was easy compared with being a slave. However, when Moses realised he should have been killed or at least grown up as a slave like those around him, he got angry with the people who kept slaves—so angry that he made a massive mistake and killed an Egyptian. That wasn't enough and Moses followed it up by making another one: he ran away. It's after all of this that God gives Moses one of the most precious gifts he could—a family and with it a wife, a new home, a job and love. God had every right to be angry with Moses but, instead of punishing him, he poured out his love to him.

Bible: 1 Samuel 16:7 (*THE MESSAGE*): But God told Samuel, 'Looks aren't everything. Don't be impressed with his looks and stature. I've already eliminated him. God judges people differently than humans do. Men and women look at the face; God looks into the heart.'

It's so easy to judge people. We don't see what is going on in other people's heads or hearts and so we base our opinion solely on what they've done. Sometimes, we even rate them based on which sins they have committed. God doesn't work like that. He doesn't rate sins; he hates all of them. God's viewpoint is different and his priorities are too. He doesn't look at what you do but who you are, when making his decisions. He sees the wonderful child he created, not the mistakes we might make.

Application: If Moses' story had stopped there, we'd have all understood. Who would choose a murderer to save anyone, let alone an entire nation? It's a good job for Moses that God doesn't work like that. He saw Moses' heart and knew one day he'd be ready and, while he waited, he kept Moses safe. He gave him a home and a family and walked with him every day as Moses did his job. We all do things we're not proud of. We all make mistakes that should cause God to leave us alone and abandon us, but we can be confident he won't ever treat us that way, even if the world tells us we deserve it. No matter what, he's going to love us, protect us and walk with us forever, and he has a job for us; he's just waiting to give it to us. We need to choose to accept God's friendship. Today we're going to take the time to give us all the opportunity to say, 'God, I want to be your friend and walk with you in my life.'

Ministry: How would you naturally respond to God's message? How can you enable the children to join you and respond in that way too?

Finding balance

Before we get to that, however, it is worth flagging up the big picture again. I believe we need to take each term as a marathon and feel the joy of small steps of teaching truths and topics. Twelve sessions on Moses give us the opportunity to look at the collection of small moments and lessons that make up his big picture, rather than covering just the highlights in one or two sessions. We don't have to teach the whole Bible by the end of the month. We are partnering with the congregation who have the ability to learn on their own or as part of their family too. It's not up to us to set out programmes that give them everything they need.

Spending longer on smaller sections also increases our need to prioritise variety from term to term. When it comes to the whole year of teaching (especially in children's and youth church) I try to keep a balance of teaching sources. While I always aim to discern prophetically the subjects we need to cover each term, as I plan term by term, the format and source of the root inspiration is more formulaic for me.

When it comes to finding the balance over an entire year, I try to spend one term a year seeking to claim the secular world for the heavenly and use a series or a full film to be the illustration for my teaching material. This is often placed during the term at the point when our new, and therefore youngest, members have just moved up into the group from their previous one. For example, we had a series called 'The gospel according to movies', in which I used twelve different films to illustrate twelve different truths that God had made clear he wanted our teenagers to understand and investigate. Our series 'Let's wreck it, Ralph!' took an adult home-group teaching series written for our church, and broke it down into ten sessions for kids' church. A whole term of watching the film *Wreck-it Ralph* clip by clip, as part of church, has been a great tool in training our young people to find God in everything and live in freedom. It has resulted in many coming back from cinema trips to exclaim, 'I found him! He was in the film and it was amazing.' It meant I could invite those who found him to teach their group what they had discovered, using their own illustrations.

Each year I also spend a term using a non-fiction, theology-style book for our young people and congregations. Books like *Can You Hear Me?: Tuning in to the God who speaks* by Brad Jersak (Monarch, 2006), or *Messy Spirituality* by Mike Yaconelli (Zondervan, 2007) are not out of reach for the youngest members of our churches if we put the time in to take them one point at a time. It builds confidence and trains them in how to take non-fiction books and the Bible, and study them in small enough sections that they are able to apply the transformative truths they contain into their day-to-day lives.

I also want to cover the Bible directly, and so we always spend a term studying a book, section or character of the Bible. We look at the whole of a journey of a Bible character or book as an extra illustration of God's truths (along with currently tangible contemporary illustrations) and use more isolated verses from other areas of the Bible as our Bible section. This develops our young people's Bible knowledge and also the way they understand and interact with the Bible and how it, in turn, interacts with itself and them.

You may share out your year of teaching in a different way, and that is great. You may do smaller series and fit more in, or do something completely different, because that is how God is calling you to work. For me, the key is balance and variety, driven by the prophetic touch of God's truth impacting on his people. As with everything, follow what God is saying to you first! This way of thinking isn't just for children and youth; it can work for adults too. The concerted, balanced effort can bring a cohesive and important year of teaching about God to his older children as well.

Using prewritten material

This model of teaching can also be used as a way of taking prewritten material and turning it into a talk or a set of talks. Daily devotionals can easily fit this breakdown, and knowing the four stages you want to cover (point, illustration, Bible, application) can help you pick out from a larger resource the aspects that you want to cover and 'borrow'. In the past, instead of writing teaching material for a topic, I have asked my leaders to use someone else's and created for them a guide of 'How to teach from this material'. I have found devotionals, especially ones with regular titled sections for each day, great for this, as I can simply say, 'Use section A as the inspiration for your point; section 3 covers your Bible passage and explanation; the 'Heart' section would make an amazing exploration slot; and the thought for the day will make a good application point.' As long as you equip your teachers well, they can follow prewritten material and still fit the format of how you would want the material covered. When it comes to how to lead the ministry part of the plan, the questions 'How would you naturally respond to God's message?', 'How can you enable the children to join you and respond in that way too?' still apply, and so the prewritten material you use doesn't need to contain any more than your written material would.

As teachers and leaders, we can often find ourselves with set ideas of what we want to happen, and the temptation is to become prescriptive and controlling in the pursuit of perfection. God chose to use people, and people aren't perfect. As his leaders, he is asking us to do the same. We may get worried that the one teaching session that gets lost to a tangential ramble will derail our whole plan, but the truth is that God is bigger than that. When we hand our material over to our leaders and helpers, we need to offer it freely and openly (just like a prophetic word given to someone we're praying for) and let them interpret and expand on it. If we care for our teams and spend our time supporting and raising them up, then we are growing teachers who can safely handle our plans.

Thinking differently:
questions to consider

Below is a list of several different aspects of the Blended approach, and questions designed to keep your brain thinking and your heart dreaming. I hope it will serve as a thought-jogger, process-developer and clarity-provider.

Dreaming and building vision is the joy of a leader. Opening ourselves up to God's speaking into the very fibres of our church is an exciting and daunting process all at once. These four aspects ('Vision', 'Communication', 'Building Blended' and 'Blended ministry') take time, consideration and heavenly input to process well, and we should be transformed by God in the process. Implementing these ideas and challenges takes more than just us—it takes team, it takes family and it takes God's direction. We aren't pioneering a solution to a problem; we are pioneering with our family for the glory of God.

Take time, ponder and pray.

Involve people, inspire and dream.

Vision

- How do you function as a church family? Do you put family first?
- Where does the 'Blender effect' fear hit your church (see pp. 30–31)?

- What does a beautiful family look like to you?
- How are you called to DISCIPLE God's people? What opportunities are you wanting to provide for your family?
- How are you called to REACH OUT to God's people? Who are you reaching now, and who are you missing?
- How are you called to RELEASE POTENTIAL in the members of your church? How are you raising leaders, and are you raising leaders of all ages?

Communication

- How are you working with God? Are you seeking him first?
- How are you enabling others to engage with the ideas of being a Blended Church?
- How are you working with your team? Are you letting them have an input in your plans?
- What does being a Blended Church mean to your existing church family?
- What will being Blended mean for your wider community?
- How are you going to communicate a clear Blended vision systematically and progressively over time?

Building Blended

Language

- Where are the inequalities in your descriptions of people's leadership roles (kids' workers, pastors, vicars, and so on)
- How do you label each activity you run? Does the name speak for itself? Is continuity evident over different age

groupings (for example, for Sunday morning activities/services/church)?

- How do you bring equality to the language surrounding each age group?
- How do you communicate the hoped-for opportunity of each activity (discipleship, outreach, releasing potential)?
- How does your vision positively manifest itself in the everyday language of the church family?
- What needs to change so that your Blended values are exhibited across the full width of your church ministry?

Training apart to be together

- Children (and their programmes): Where are your weak spots?
- Youth (and their programmes): Where are you struggling?
- Adults (and their programmes): Where are you stale and where do you need new inspiration?
- What do you have to learn from your children?
- What do you have to learn from your youth?
- What do you have to learn from your adults?

Team and leadership

- How are you growing as a church?
- Do you have a culture that breeds leadership and depth of relationship?
- Does the body of the church understand their call into leadership?
- How are you growing everyone as a supportive crowd of witnesses to every area of church life?
- How are you giving your 'full face' to your teams?
- Are you doing yourself out of a job?

Blended ministry

All

- Does your vision for each opportunity (discipleship, reaching out, releasing potential) look the same and have the same value for each age range of your church family?
- Does every age have influence over each age's ministry?
- Do you listen to each other before planning something new?
- Do you have the deep-rooted belief that you can meet with God when everyone is 'in the room' together?

The building blocks

- How are you building community in your church family?
- How is your formatting building up good heavenly habits?
- How are you intentionally providing discipleship for all of your church family, corporately, in age groups and individually?
- How are you encouraging everyone to put their passion into action and live missionally?

Worship

- Do you have a Blended songbook?
- Do you have corporate ways of preparing to worship?
- How are you going to champion individuality in worship?
- How are you providing for variety in your worship opportunities?

Teaching

- Does your vision for what is being taught include every age?

- Are you working on learning how to learn together as well as how to teach a Blended congregation?
- Are you seeking a good balance of finding God in his word, in the world and in our lives?
- Is your teaching tangible and practical?

Encountering the Holy Spirit

- Do you expect God to turn up?
- Do you teach about the Holy Spirit with expectancy?
- Do you use the uniqueness of each leader and their own ways of meeting God to bring variety to your programmes?
- Are you valuing creativity and experimentation?

Core Skills for Family Ministry

User-friendly modular training course for children's and family work practitioners

Core Skills is an interdenominational modular scheme offering foundational training for all those involved with church-based family ministry.

It offers six stand-alone sessions on:

- Biblical, historical and contemporary understanding of family
- Family ministry today
- Seasons of family life
- Role of family relationships
- Family wellbeing and wholeness
- Faith in families

All six modules have been field-tested as pilot sessions with participants from different denominations. Each module is creative, thought-provoking, interactive and designed to inspire and refresh children's and family workers at all levels of expertise and experience.

ISBN 978 0 85746 431 6   £12.99

Parenting Children for a Life of Confidence

Rachel Turner

'The world has a formula for confidence. It goes like this:

You are amazing and perfect, just the way you are. People should love and accept you, and if they don't, well, that's their problem.

Some of the Christian community goes along with this formula. We can be told in church:

God made you perfect and precious. You are unique and wonderful, like a gemstone in his eyes, worthy of so much.

We think that if our children could just believe those statements deep in their hearts, then they would be confident. The problem is that it doesn't seem to be working.'

In this thought-provoking and engaging book Rachel Turner explores how we can help our children to discover a healthy core of confidence, offering practical wisdom and suggestions for nurturing this in daily life.

ISBN 978 0 85746 167 4   £8.99
Also available for Kindle

The Barnabas Family Bible

Bible reading fun for all the family!

The Barnabas Family Bible is written for parents, grandparents and carers to share with their children through an interactive family Bible and prayer time. It spans the whole Bible narrative through 110 key extracts, with each section providing a brief comment on the passage, questions to discuss, a visual aid to encourage engagement with the story, an activity idea, a prayer idea, a key verse and an Old or New Testament story link.

Also included:

- Guidance and support for sharing faith as a family
- A family-friendly overview of the Bible story
- A selection of best-loved Bible passages
- Further resources to support families and family Bible study

ISBN 978 0 84101 713 6 · £9.99

Enjoyed

this book?

Write a review–we'd love to hear what you think.
Email: reviews@brf.org.uk

Keep up to date–receive details of our new books as they happen.
Sign up for email news and select your interest groups at:
www.brfonline.org.uk/findoutmore/

Follow us on Twitter @brfonline

By post–to receive new title information by post (UK only), complete
the form below and post to: BRF Mailing Lists, 15 The Chambers, Vineyard,
Abingdon, Oxfordshire, OX14 3FE

Your Details
Name _____
Address_____
_____
Town/City _____ Post Code _____
Email_____

Your Interest Groups (*Please tick as appropriate)	
☐ Advent/Lent	☐ Messy Church
☐ Bible Reading & Study	☐ Pastoral
☐ Children's Books	☐ Prayer & Spirituality
☐ Discipleship	☐ Resources for Children's Church
☐ Leadership	☐ Resources for Schools

Support your local bookshop
Ask about their new title information schemes.